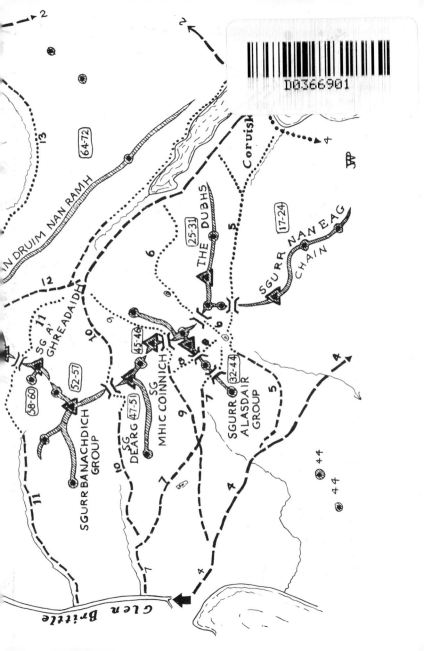

SCRAMBLES IN SKYE

Sg.Alasdair and the Great Stone Shoot.
Sg.Mhic Coinnich on the left.

SCRAMBLES IN SKYE

A GUIDE TO WALKS AND SCRAMBLES IN THE BLACK CUILLIN

by J.Wilson Parker

Diagrams and maps by the author
Photographs by C.R.Haigh

CICERONE PRESS
MILNTHORPE, CUMBRIA

© J. Wilson Parker 1983
First published 1983
Reprinted 1985, 1988, 1992
Revised 1995, Reprinted 1998

ISBN 0 902363 38 7

Front cover:
Sgurr Mhic Coinnich in the foreground
Sgurr nan Gillean in the distance

Back cover:
Snow lingers in Coir' a' Ghrundda in early June

Photos: R.B.Evans

Biographical Note

Since leaving school John Parker worked for the Ordnance Survey as a cartographic surveyor. When based in the Lake District & the Yorkshire Dales he was involved in climbing and mountain rescue. His visits to the Cuillin began in 1971. He and his wife recently retired to Grange-over-Sands.

Acknowledgement

The author wishes to record his appreciation of John Howard Collins for his support, advice and shared enthusiasm for the Cuillin Hills.

CONTENTS

SCRAMBLING IS DANGEROUS

Part of the Cuillin's appeal is the adventure and potential danger inherent in mountain activities. The reader should bear in mind that any of the routes described in this guide can become difficult and hazardous due to changing weather which can suddenly alter the condition of the rocks or curtail visibility. The consequences of an error in navigation, an uncontrolled slide or unprotected fall are usually severe and can be fatal. Parties of walkers or climbers can only judge for themselves the viability and safety of each and every step of their proposed route as they climb up or down. Most accidents occur in descent when parties are tired or anxious. Unlike other British mountains there are few easy ways off the Cuillin Hills and no easy-way-round is available when difficulties occur.

INTRODUCTION

The Peaks of the Cuillin constitute the only range in Britain where rock-climbing and mountaineering techniques are required to reach many of the summits. The pioneers not only claimed first ascents of virgin peaks but also enjoyed the opportunity of christening several of their conquests and intervening passes. Today the Cuillin remain the Mecca of the British climber.

This guide attempts to indicate the summits the rambler and scrambler can attain, or where the rope is required by the mountaineer bound for more difficult peaks. Descriptions are limited to the main, natural approaches, the book not purporting to be a rock-climbing guide. Every worth-while rock-climb made on the Isle of Skye has been described generally, or in detail if necessary, in the Scottish Mountaineering Club Climbers' Guide Books.

The Main Ridge is described broadly group by group from south to north. Each group is named after the presiding 'Munro'. In the original tables compiled by Sir Hugh T. Munro in 1891 only nine 3,000 foot mountains were listed. Today there are twelve including Blaven. One group is entitled 'An Druim nan Ramh' but does not contain a peak above the 3,000 criterion. Bidein Druim nan Ramh, a complex and difficult peak, stands athwart a long traverse ridge to which neither of its higher neighbours deserves a claim. Peaks within their groups are described in geographical order from south to north. The easiest way is dealt with first.

Many will wish to spend their day traversing the MAIN RIDGE over several peaks. Climbers maintain that the complete traverse provides the finest expedition in Britain. With this in mind those portions of any route constituting a section of the Main Ridge or a necessary variation for walking parties will be sidelined as shown -

  ↟ indicates the route is described south to north

  ↡ indicates the route is described north to south.

Grading System

1W	Easy fell-walking on good paths or easy terrain.
2W	Strenuous walking over steep and rough terrain.
3S	Some easy scrambling with little exposure.
4S	Exposed or strenuous scrambles: a rope not required by experienced parties in normal conditions. Otherwise a

proficient leader with a rope is recommended as a stand-by.

RI   Easy rock-climbing.

RII   Rock climbs graded Moderate - often very exposed.

RIII   Rock climbs graded Difficult.

RIV   Rock climbs graded Very Difficult or harder.

Distances and Heights

Distances are expressed in miles and furlongs:

8 furlongs	=	1 mile
1 furlong	=	0.2 kilometres
1.6 kilometres	=	1 mile
1 kilometre	=	5 furlongs

Heights are expressed in feet:

One foot	=	0.3048 metres
One metre	=	3.2808 feet

For metric heights of peaks on the Main Ridge refer to
Appendix II.

Access

There is no stalking or other forms of 'sport' in the Cuillin and
thanks to the goodwill of the principal 'lairds' - The Clan McLeod
of Dunvegan and the proprietor of Camasunary there is no
hindrance to the.climber. It is interesting to recall that the McLeods
once insisted that climbing parties employed one of the guides who
were quartered in bothies once standing on the highroad west from
Sligachan.

Equipment & Safety

Give at least some idea of your intentions. It will be comforting to
the lost or injured to know somebody at base can advise Mountain
Rescue teams where overdue parties had headed. Conversely the
police, ghillies, shepherds and climbers who may spend up to a week-
often in weather in which they would not choose to operate -
combing ravines and other dangerous places will not be overjoyed to
learn the 'bodies' turned up at home after an unannounced change
of heart!

Due to the magnetic nature of the rocks our ally, the **COMPASS** is only useful in the Cuillin if used with care. They are notoriously 'led astray' on summits and ridges but recover their efficacy after one has come down some way off the ridge when you can verify your direction. Experiment will indicate in which type of terrain one can obtain reliable bearings by comparing visual sightings with a map bearing in clear conditions. General advice is: keep clear of pinnacles and cairns. Remove compass from solid rocks. Repeat compass readings at several points at least ten yards apart and if they agree within 10 degrees accept the mean result as a reasonable answer.

The Skye **MOUNTAIN RESCUE** team is based on the Police Station at Portree (Tel Portree 2888). Public call boxes are situated at Sligachan Hotel, Glenbrittle House, Elgol, Torrin and Luib.

Weather

Skye is known to the Gaels as Eilean a'Cheo - The Isle of Mist. Every 'Skyeman' knows rain can prevail at any time of the year. May and June are statistically the least wet months. Midges can make a camp or bivouac unendurable between May and September. If a climbing party is afflicted by poor weather they can find solace in other parts of the 'Magic Isle', which offers a wealth of varied excursions.

Walkers and scramblers should never attempt to force a route in mist but retreat if it proves persistent. Roped climbing parties may prefer to complete their route but should select the least complicated return to base.

Winter conditions are neither enduring nor reliable but demand Alpine equipment and techniques. Suffice to add that winter days in this latitude are dangerously short and necessitate fast movement born of experience and confidence.

p.9-12
A Select Bibliography
Books currently in print include:-

Scottish Mountaineering Club produce definitive guides:-

Rock & Ice Climbs in Skye, J.R. Mackenzie

Islands of Scotland District Guide

Ernest Press:-

> *The Cuillin of Skye* (reprint), H.B. Humble
> *The History of Mountain Activities*

Constable:-

> *Magic of Skye,* W.A. Poucher
> (For walking and scrambling)

Collins New Naturalist Series:-

> *The Highlands and Islands,*
> F.Fraser Darling & J.Morton Boyd

Collins Companion Guides:-

> *The Western Highlands and Islands,*
> W.H. Murray (general guide)

Her Majesty's Stationery Office:-

> *Regional Geological Handbook* - Tertiary
> *Volcanic Districts, Institute of Geological Sciences*

The Way to the Cuillin

Your local travel agent/railway station should provide information regarding public transport to, and on the island. Each year Farm Holiday Guides Ltd., Abbey Mill Centre, Paisley, PA1 1JN, publishes a comprehensive timetable of all land, sea and air services in the Highlands and Islands of Scotland.

Among those railways continually under threat of the 'axe' are the two that connect Fort William with Mallaig and Inverness to Kyle of Lochalsh.

Scottish Citylink express coaches connect Glasgow etc., to Kyle and Portree. Scottish Citylink, Buchanan Bus Station, Glasgow G2 3NP Tel: 0141 332 9191

Services run by Highland Scottish Omnibuses Ltd., Seafield Road, Inverness Tel: 01463 233371 and Sutherland's Bus Service, Carbost Tel: 0147 842 267/310 serve the south of the Island.

Motorists

Motorists 'furth o' the Border' will find a convenient route to Kyle of Lochalsh is: M6, M74, M73, M80, M9, A84, A85, A87 that is Carlisle

- Hamilton - Stirling - Callander - Crianlarich - Fort William (last halt for supplies, climbing gear and cheap petrol) - Glen Shiel - Kyle.

Skye ceased to be an island on completion of The Bridge (toll) during autumn 1995.

The Island's well-engineered 'A' roads lead to Sligachan and Drynoch. The minor road over to, and down Glen Brittle is narrow and winds about a great deal. Unfortunately, the surface is now tarred and the old watersplashes have been superseded by bridges.

An alternative and beautiful approach to Skye can be made by branching off the A87 at Shiel Bridge and crossing the Man Ratagan to Glenelg, enjoying the classic view of the Five Sisters of Kintail from the hairpin stretch. The small ferry to Kylerhea does not operate between early September and late May nor on Sundays but in the week battles with the quarter-mile of tidal waters between 0900-1700 hours. The road thence to Broadford crossing Bealach Udal is, at 960 feet, the highest public thoroughfare on Skye. (Tel: 01599 511302)

The most romantic route is that of 'The Road to the Isles': the A830. This busy road runs to Mallaig from Fort William. A car-carrying steamer operated by Caledonian MacBrayne departs five times a day for Armadale pier between 0800 and 1900 hours, and takes half an hour to cross the Sound of Sleat. The return sailings for Mallaig are 0900 2000. (Tel: 01687 462403)

The Accommodation

As will be anticipated on the Isles and in the Highlands a hillgoer with a tent enjoys the greatest choice of centre. One may camp out of sight and sound of civilisation but safety demands that you indulge in a wild site in the company of experienced mountaineers.

SLIGACHAN the traditional climbers' centre is now a complex catering for most tastes and pockets with its famous hotel, Alltdaraich self-catering chalets and a campsite with all facilities and a shop Tel: 047852 204/313.

CARBOST has a store/post office, petrol, a bar and self-catering.

PORTNALONG harbours a climbers' bunkhouse Tel: 01478 640254.

GLENBRITTLE offers self-catering but guides and accommodation may be sought at Stac Lee, Tel: 01478 640289. The youth hostel (Tel: 01478 640278) has a shop within its custom-built timber walls and is closed in the winter. The shop at the campsite sells food, maps etc. to the public. Finally the Memorial Hut administered by the British Mountaineering Council is used by its members as a wardened, self-catering establishment.

PORTREE, the capital, has a Tourist Information Centre (Tel: 01478 612137) worth visiting on an off day while others look round the gift shops or cash cheques. Hotels, pubs, guest houses and one basic campsite and another despoiled by caravans provide a variety of accommodation.

BROADFORD also has an information centre (Tel: 01471 822361) plus identical, if smaller, choice of facilities, but is handier for Blaven and boasts a youth hostel (Tel: 01471 822442).

CAMASUNARY and LOCH SCAVAIG can only be reached on foot or by boat from Elgol (or Glenbrittle). At the west end of the meadows nearest the footbridge at Camasunary stands a bothy which provides primitive shelter for back-packers. The Memorial Hut on the shore of Loch Scavaig provides the perfect base for a climbing holiday, away from it all. It is run by the Junior Mountaineering Club of Scotland and contains 6 bunks and cooking facilities. The landing stage lies close to the hut. Parties staying here could be cut off by bad weather.

TORRIN and ELGOL have post office/shops, guest houses and telephone boxes. The famed calendar view from the shore at Elgol provides the most dramatic introduction to that most spectacular range of hills.

The Rocks
A basic understanding of the composition and formation of the rocks constituting the Cuillin will be of help to the climber or rambler during his excursions onto the Ridge and add some interest to visits in the area. Sheets 70E and 71W of the 1:50,000 Geological Survey maps are informative. They were largely the result of the labours of Alfred Harker in the early years of this century. Solid and Drift editions are both available. The one-inch sheets are superseded.

The whole of Skye consists of a variety of rocks built on a 2½ mile thick platform of an ancient (600 plus million years old) granite compressed into GNEISS and SCHIST, though Soay to the south differs in being built of a coarse variety of TORRIDONIAN SANDSTONE.

A complete series of volcanic eruptions during the Tertiary epoch which began 70 million years ago built up the Cuillin we see today. A widespread up-welling of lavas through countless fissures in the gneiss and schist started the volcanic activity. These lavas spread over the surface and settled into sheets between 20 and 100 feet thick separated by layers of slag, to a depth of 1,000 feet, extending south to Ireland and as far north as Greenland. Because the lava cooled at or near the surface their crystals are tiny, indeed invisible. The cooling action also resulted in the characteristic hexagonal vertical joints which produced for example the famous columnar formations at the Giant's Causeway and Fingal's Cave. These dark and heavy rocks - BASALT are included among the Basic (quartz-free) igneous rocks. Today the eroded margins of the basalt form the vertical sea-cliffs above Loch Brittle and the Sound of Soay. The plateau circling the western approaches to the Cuillin consists of this rock and displays a stepped appearance thanks to the horizontal flow of the lavas. A layer of peat blankets these areas, and with long grass soon erodes the water resistance in climbing boots. This otherwise featureless plateau is relieved by deep ravines which streams have eroded along the courses of the 'DYKES'. The upwelling of lava can result in various subterranean formations. Walls of lava formed in vertical fissures are known as dykes. Depending on the variation of resistance to weathering of the rocks involved, subsequent erosion at the surface can form either ravines and gullies or walls. SILLS are horizontal fillings of hard volcanic rock sandwiched between rock layers. LACCOLITHS are domes of lava pushing the layers of rock into an arch but spreading horizontally across the floor of an unyielding lower strata. BATHOLITHS are similar but bottomless.

The next stage in the formation of our mountains comprised a second welling of basic lava, but this time deep beneath the surface laccoliths of basic lava formed and cooled slowly under the weight of the basalt, and became the coarse-grained PERIDOTITE and GABBRO which constitute the major part of the Main Ridge.

PERIDOTITE was the result of the first of these underground intrusions and is the coarsest of basic rocks. It was subsequently enveloped by the great masses of GABBRO. This rock, the prevalent constituent of the Cuillin, allows little vegetation to colonise its surface. Though known as the BLACK Cuillin these rocks are almost chameleon-like, adopting both sanguine and steely hues. Ragged garments, scratched boots and hands bear mute testimony to the roughness of gabbro and peridotite.

Some BASALT was also enveloped in the laccoliths and was baked hard, smooth and brittle. Unlike the later basalt intrusions it has survived its blanket of gabbro to form the highest peaks, including Sgùrr Alasdair. Few belays are to be found on this area.

East of Glen Sligachan the batholiths of an 'acid' lava (acid rocks contain quartz) cooled slowly and formed GRANOPHYRE, a type of granite.

Millions of years' erosion eventually stripped the original covering of basalt and exposed both the gabbro and granophyre. The latter decomposes into a gravel - not so the gabbro. This rock weathers by the ton, creating the tortured sky-line of the Black Cuillin, in total contrast to the regular conical slopes of the Red Cuillin. Gabbro provides a hard and rough surface but remember the process of disintegration is still in hand. Make sure that hand is not your own when by-passing the numerous and often massive blocks lying in wait for the unwary. Ledges abound with debris; neat footwork and considerate rope management is essential for the safety of those below.

Continued volcanic activity caused further minor intrusions. BASALT DYKES were formed in the gabbro when it split. These weathered and today form the beds of the gullies cutting the Main Ridge both squarely and acutely. Although a smooth rock, the basalt breaks into steps and often allows easy ways through otherwise difficult and slabby areas.

SILLS or CONE-SHEETS of QUARTZ-DOLERITE, a fine-grained material, were intruded into and stratified the gabbro. The resulting dip in the rocks runs towards and becomes steeper near an imaginary centre in the area of Loch Coruisk. This stratification has led to the western side of the Main Ridge displaying a series of ledges in contrast to the slabby east faces. On sections of the Ridge (particularly where it turns east at Sgurr a' Mhadaidh) are wave-like formations where layers of gabbro have gone creating steps and false ridges which make route-finding complicated in mist.

Much more recently, but still thousands of years ago, during the Ice Ages glaciers flowed from the upper corries down the glens into the sea and affected the landscape profoundly. Rocks on the flanks and floors of the valleys were ground smooth, making present-day access to some corries difficult i.e. Coir' an Lochain. Glacial erosion also formed a few rock basins presently occupied by pools. The prime example is Loch Coruisk which is some 200 feet deep. Frost action continues to be responsible for the scree and boulders which fill the beds of some corries but provide easy though trying routes to gaps in the ridges.

The above notes should explain why a day on the Cuillin begins with a bog-trot over moorland cut by the occasional ravine. A climb up slabs leads to an elevated hollow filled with rock debris surrounding a small pool. A scree-shoot reaches a square-cut gap in the skyline whence a scramble along a narrow ridge avoiding steps by slabs or ledges completes the ascent of an airy summit.

Details of the structure of individual mountains can be found in the introduction to each peak.

The Pioneers

No introduction to the Cuillin would be complete without some reference to the men who discovered the attractions and made the first ascents of these hills a century ago or more.

1810-19 The geologist Dr. JOHN MACCULLOUGH attempts to reach the summits.

1814 Sir Walter Scott visits Coruisk.

1835 The first scramble on record. A local forester DUNCAN MACINTYRE and the Reverend LESINGHAM SMITH visit Coruisk and return to Sligachan over the difficult Druim nan Ramh.

1836 A difficult peak is climbed. On July 7th DUNCAN MACINTYRE leads scientist JAMES FORBES via the 'Tourist Route' to the summit of **SGÙRR NAN GILLEAN.**

1845 Professor FORBES, a pioneer glaciologist, while preparing the first map, of the 'Cuchullin Hills' compares the height of **BRUACH NA FRITHE** and Sgùrr nan Gillean with a barometer, ascending the latter this time from the south. (Many visitors are guided to Gillean's summit in the mid

15

19th century by local ghillies).

1857 Professor JOHN NICOL and the poet ALGERNON SWINBURNE ascend the easy south ridge of **BLAVEN**

1859 An Alpine Club member C.R. WELD visits **SGÙRR NA STRI** and is impressed by the Inaccessible Pinnacle recently included on the Admiralty Chart. Little heed is paid to his challenging description of the Cuillin.

1865 Sees the start of a long campaign by a native of Skye, Sherrif ALEXANDER NICOLSON (1827-93). With MacIntyre's son descends the West Ridge of Gillean via eponymous chimney.

1870 14 year old JOHN MACKENZIE born Sconsor begins a lengthy & famous guiding career, accompanying W. Tribe to the top of **SGÙRR A' GHREADAIDH.**

1871 Four army officers visit **SGÙRR DUBH BEAG.**

1873 A noteworthy year. Local guide, MACPHERSON is bribed by PROFESSOR KNIGHT to accompany him to the top of 'the Little Horn', now **KNIGHT'S PEAK** on the Pinnacle Ridge of Gillean.

ALEXANDER NICOLSON bags **SGÙRR NA BANA-CHDICH** and **SGÙRR DEARG** with JOHN MACKEN-ZIE. Their season is crowned by the first ascent of the Cuillin's highest peak which was then regarded as part of Sgùrr Sgumain and since named after Alexander;- **SGÙRR ALASDAIR.**

1874 Finds the 'home team' of NICOLSON and MACKENZIE making a **descent** of **SGÙRR DUBH MÒR** in darkness to Coir' an Lochain without a rope! This tour de force is one the author would urge the reader **not** to emulate.

1880 Another strong team or 'rope' enters the lists - brothers LAWRENCE and CHARLES PILKINGTON. Since they made their first (fishing) trip to Skye eight years before, they have several alpine seasons under their belts and have become the leading climbers of their time. 1880 must be a poor 'sporting season' so their attention is turned to the lowly peaks of the Cuillin. To their chagrin a frontal assault on Gillean is repulsed! An attempt on the West Ridge succeeds and another pair of 'Skyemen' are inspired. In fact Weld's challenge is taken up that very year and the 18th August finds them robbing Sgùrr Dearg's **PINNACLE** of its **IN-ACCESSIBILITY!** Gillean's **PINNACLE RIDGE** is another important climb.

1883　LAWRENCE PILKINGTON with HULTON and WALKER ascends **BIDEIN DRUIM NAN RAMH.**

1884　During a 'wet' season with HORACE WALKER and HULTON, J. HEELIS and the redoubtable guide John Mackenzie, CHARLES PILKINGTON returns to bag his own **SGÙRR THEARLAICH** by its western face plus the guide's **SGÙRR MHIC COINNICH** over the north ridge. His other first ascents with Mackenzie are **SGÙRR NA'H UAMHA** 1887 and **CLACH GLAS** 1888.

1887　Professor NORMAN COLLIE visits the island - for the fishing....he sees Rev. A.H. STOCKER and J.A. PARKER putting up a new route on Knight's Peak shortly after their first ascent of the WEST RIDGE of the 'INN PINN'. The inspired scientist picks their brains and telegraphs for a rope. After failing on both Gillean's Pinnacle and West Ridges, JOHN MACKENZIE conducts COLLIE to the top via the Tourist Route! Thus begins a lifelong affair with mountains taking him to the far corners of the globe, though each summer of a long life is spent in sight at least of the Cuillin! With John Mackenzie as his constant companion, he discovers **COLLIE'S LEDGE on MHIC COINNICH** and that Alasdair is higher than Dearg and therefore the 'king' of the Cuillin.

1889　The Scottish Mountaineering Club conceived by W.W. NAISMITH. Collie reaches the summit of the **BASTEIR TOOTH** alone!

1891　Sir HUGH MUNRO publishes his tables which enumerate nine mountains and three 'tops' in Skye. The S.M.C. holds a meet in the Cuillin. The **THEARLAICH-DUBH GAP** crossed by COLLIE, KING and MACKENZIE.

1896　The last virgin mountain to be climbed in Britain is ascended via its most difficult North Face - **SGÙRR COIR' AN LOCHAIN** BY COLLIE, HOWELL, NAISMITH and MACKENZIE. COLLIE and HOWELL also effect the longest rock-climb yet undertaken, the **SOUTH-EAST RIDGE of SGÙRR A'GHREADAIDH** and the airy **NORTH FACE** of **ALASDAIR** with NAISMITH and PHILIP.

17

1898	The remaining problems of the Main Ridge are overcome. KING, NAISMITH and WILLIAM DOUGLAS climb directly to **SGÙRR MHIC CHOINNICH** from the bealach via **KING'S CHIMNEY** then NAISMITH and A.M. MACKAY overcome that most intimidating direct ascent of the **TOOTH** from Bealach nan Lice.
1906	A photograph taken seven years before indicated the presence of the **CIOCH** on the precipice of **SRÒN NA CICHE.** COLLIE finally reaches this pinnacle with MACKENZIE and pioneers the first route on a cliff now riven with a network of popular climbs.
1907	The S.M.C's Journal is devoted to a Mountaineer's Guide to Skye.
1908	'The Keswick Brothers' ASHLEY and GEORGE ABRAHAM produce the first climbing book about the Cuillin - 'Rock Climbing in Skye'.
1911	Sees the first complete traverse of the MAIN RIDGE by LESLIE SHADBOLT and A.C. MACLAREN.
1923	The S.M.C. Guide to Skye includes many new climbs made by STEEPLE and BARLOW. DR BARLOW'S OUTLINE MAP published.
1939	**THE GREATER TRAVERSE** of the Main Ridge plus CLACH GLAS and BLAVEN is accomplished by IAN CHARLESON and W.E. FORDE.
1945	'THE MAGIC OF SKYE' a magnificent photographic record by W.A. POUCHER is published.
1965	FIRST WINTER TRAVERSE over two days is made by DAVID CRABBE, BRIAN ROBERTSON, TOM PATEY and HAMISH MACINNES. Ordnance Survey publish accurate 6 inch map based on Aerial Survey techniques.

18

The Paths

1. SLIGACHAN - GLENBRITTLE Easy walking 1W
8 miles 1,200 feet of Ascent (inc. 4 miles of road-walking)

From the Hotel follow the A863 towards Drynoch for 5-600 yards.
Parking is possible on north side of road. An un-tarred road on the
left leads through a gate to the old Keeper's cottage - Allt Dearg
House, a white-washed dwelling standing on the open peaty moor. A
boggy track avoids this fenced property on the right before rejoining
the old well-marked path following the left (NW) bank of the cas-
cading Allt Dearg Mór or Red Burn. This leads gently up into the
shallow depression of Coire na Circe set among open heath. At
intervals the Burn falls into dark pools. The summit of the Màm
(3mls 1,150ft) is marked by a pool drained by the Allt a'Mhaim
which in its turn conducts our path on the steady descent to the road
in Glenbrittle.

Passing a well constructed cairn the path divides for a short
distance then meanders across the slopes past the corner of a forest
fence on the right. You are now in Coire na Creiche named after a
fierce struggle between the McLeods and McDonalds long ago in
1601. Some authorities maintain its name signifies a place where
robbers gathered to exchange their winnings.

On the Sligachan side of our pass the central attraction on an ex-
ceptionally broken skyline was the axe-shaped Basteir Tooth. Now
the view south to the Cuillin comprises a rocky headwall from which
the conical peak of the Water-pipe protrudes dividing the Coire into
two upper branches now correctly named Coir'a'Tarneilear (left) and
Coir' a'Mhadaidh (right) instead of inter-posed on maps and guides as
before the mid-sixties. The Allt a'Mhaim tumbles more steeply than
the path to join the burns flowing from either side of Sgùrr an
Fheadain to form the River Brittle. Our path runs across the fell-side
along a forest fence to join tarmacadam at 300 feet above the sea
(4mls 7 furlongs). This exalted altitude is the maximum that
mechanical aid may lift the walker and climber on his way to a
Cuillin top or pass. Elsewhere sea-level is one's starting point!

19

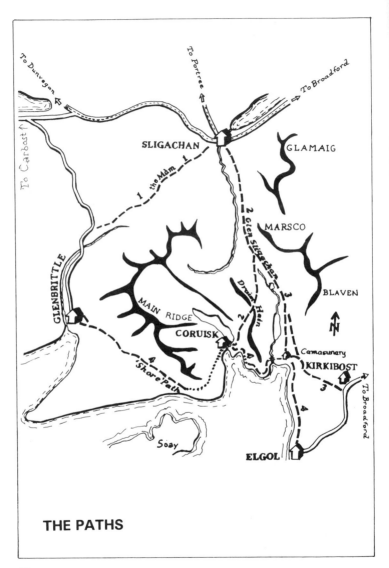

THE PATHS

Those who have no transport parked at the handy spot by a forest entrance just up-hill from the path-junction now are faced with a 2¼ml road walk along Glenbrittle Forest side to the Youth Hostel (7ml 2f). A further ½ mile brings one to the Memorial Hut and Glenbrittle House. The total distance to the Camp Site is 8 miles 3 furlongs of mainly easy going.

2. SLIGACHAN - CORUISK and LOCH SCAVAIG 2W
7 miles 3 furlongs 1,200ft of ascent. Easy walking, but difficult river crossing in wet weather.

Cross the *Old* Bridge spanning the Sligachan River and take the path to the right before the old road crosses another, smaller burn (Allt Daraich). The path runs near the Daraich until the Forester's house is passed on the opposite bank. Leaving the burn the track takes a parallel course to the river. It is well marked but proves rather stony and tedious, though it does avoid the marshier ground nearer the river. The shapely peak on the left is Marsco. After a fence one leaps or boulder-hops a stream. A boulder crowned with a tangle of roots is passed, boasting the title Clach na Craoibhe Chaoruinn (2 miles). Progressing southwards the Pinnacles on Sgùrr nan Gillean's North Ridge grow more pronounced. At 3½ miles the River Sligachan veers west while our path continues over a low watershed marked by the twin pools of Lochan Dubha. The marshland in which they lie is avoided by the path 200 yards east and 100 feet higher. Now the path divides. The left fork crosses a burn flowing from a corrie on the left and continues down the glen before eventually reaching Camasunary *(Route 3)*. The Coruisk path however stays on the right of the burn and climbs across the hillside to the south onto a flat shoulder. Still rising, a low depression is crossed to a second ridge marked by a large cairn (5 miles 7 furlongs).

Here on Druim Hain at 1,038 feet we have Coire Riabhach, Coruisk and the sea ahead and below. The way so far has been over granite. Now gabbro will be under foot. The path - now less well-marked - takes one left of the Loch and its outlet, gradually losing height to reach the shore of dark Loch Coruisk a couple of hundred yards short of the line of rounded, awkward boulders which serve as stepping-stones. Here the River Scavaig begins its 300 yard journey to the sea. Surprisingly another 'river' on the mainland can beat it for the title of Scotland's shortest! All the rain (or snow) falling into the vast rock-basin of Coir'-Uisg - literally the 'corrie of the waters' finds its way between, and often *over,* the stepping-stones. Please note that heavy rainfall renders the crossing difficult, if not dangerous. The army constructed a footbridge here some years ago, but little remained after the first winter storms. The way by shanks's pony round the Loch is 3 miles 2 furlongs but is preferable to a rapid and conclusive journey to the sea. The view of the Loch with the back-cloth of the central Cuillin must be one of the most impressive in Britain. The peak dominating the head of the basin is Sgùrr à Ghreadaidh. To both left and right, ice-worn slabs of gabbro descend to shore-level.

Having negotiated the stepping-stones follow the river down around a slabby brow of rock on the right. The path leads abruptly to the landing-stage on Loch Scavaig. Here is the scene of disembark-ation of scores of trippers during the tourist season. The Coruisk Memorial hut is tucked beneath the cliffs a hundred yards from shore and will be found by skirting the base of the rocks when the southern end is encountered.

N.B. In wet weather consider Route 12 as an alternative. (Sligachan-Hut, 9 miles 3 furlongs and 2,400 feet of ascent).

3. SLIGACHAN - CAMASUNARY - KIRKIBOST
Easy walking 1W   9 miles 2 furlongs   1,000 feet of ascent

Follow Route 2 to the path junction (3½ miles) and continue downhill between the granite slopes of Ruadh Stac and the flat wastes of Sràth na Crèitheach. At 5 miles pass Loch an Athain and enter a rock basin occupied by Loch na Crèitheach, or Creubhaich; a large lake nestling between the flanks of Sgùrr Hain and mighty Blaven, both gabbro. Closing with the N.E. corner of the loch the path forks. The left-hand path takes a more easterly course by-passing Camasunary and joining the track from Kirkibost.

The right-hand path continues along the shore passing a boathouse then crosses a low gap below An-t-Sròn 465 feet to the lonely farm buildings and bothy on either side of a green enclosure by the sea shore (7¾ miles).

Beyond Camasunary a track leads south-east over moorland over another 'Mam' 620 feet to the A881 between Elgol and Kirkibost.

See Route 4 for continuation to Elgol 1W.

4. THE 'SHORE' PATH

Glen Brittle-Coruisk
   3S rough walking and some scrambling.
   7 miles 3 furlongs   1,200 feet of ascent
Coruisk-Camasunary
   4S easy walking - moderate scramble 2 miles 7 furlongs.
   400 feet ascent
Camasunary-Elgol
   1W walking, 3 miles 2 furlongs. 700 feet ascent

   Total:- 13 miles 2 furlongs 2,300 feet of ascent.

The 'SHORE-WALK' should never be taken lightly. A heavily-laden party may require two days. Bad weather may prevent progress at any of three locations on this gruelling journey. If Elgol (or Glen Brittle) must be reached on foot during indeterminate conditions then consider going via Sligachan (*Routes 1 and 3*).

Where the tarmac fades beyond Glen Brittle House the road down the glen divides. Go straight past corrugated Cuillin Cottage and follow a path through the rough field beside the campsite. Before the shore develops a line of low cliffs, a track leads away from the sea over moorland towards Coire Làgan and the nearest peaks of the Cuillin. In half a mile the trodden way comes alongside a burn. This is crossed and a track heading S.E. passing left of a small pool continues rising steadily over rough moorland. The burn issuing from Làgan is crossed easily (1 mile 7 furlongs) and the path wanders between the wet plateau and the lower flanks of Sròn na Ciche, Sgùrr nan Eag and Gars-Bheinn. Other burns draining Coir'a'Ghrunnda (3 miles) and Coire nan Laogh (3 miles 7 furlongs) are easily crossed with a leap then our path gradually fades and re-appears as one follows a shelf high above the Sound of Soay.

5 miles from Glen Brittle one is left high and not too dry without a definite path. One can contour then climb to avoid and stay above a tier of dolerite cliffs, 600 feet above the Sound until one reaches the burn of Allt na Fraoich. Cross this and maintain height swinging north. A cairned shelf continues in this direction as far as a stream draining Coir'a'Chruidh. Below the crossing-place is a waterfall and some cliffs. Rising slightly, two small pools are encountered as one continues north along the 1,000 feet contour above Loch Scavaig. The base of a large gabbro crag comes in from the left and one is

23

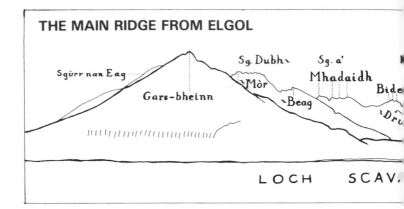

THE MAIN RIDGE FROM ELGOL

Sgùrr nan Eag

Gars-bheinn

Sg. Dubh ⌐Mòr

⌐Beag

Sg. a'
Mhadaidh

Bide

⌐Dr

L O C H   S C A V.

forced down to a smaller line of slabs which peter out leaving a way down. Now you can descend steeply to the shore under the cliffs of the Mad Burn Buttress. This is the large crag, just ahead, which holds several rock-climbs on sound gabbro in the 'severe' category.

Beyond the buttress glaciated slabs dip into the sea. To cross them the plastic water-piping supplying the Hut can be used as a 'lifeline'. Two places are tricky. Then one has a short stretch of machair before the door of the Coruisk hut is reached. 7⅓ miles.

Retracing our path to a point a mile east of the crossing of Allt Coire nan Laogh, a small stream crosses the last vestiges of the path from Glen Brittle. Here an alternative route can be taken to Coruisk. Descend diagonally right to the shore at Point of Ulfhart. A waymarked route uses an ancient wave platform of marsh and rock above the shallow cliffs to join the route previously described, below Mad Burn Buttress. This way might be a little longer but is less complicated.

The second section of the journey begins with the crossing of the Scavaig. A path from the hut joins that from the landing steps and rounds the smooth gabbro spur of Meall nan Cuilce. The river is followed upstream to its outflow from Loch Coruisk and a crossing effected of the line of rounded boulders that constitute the stepping-stones. In heavy rain these may be rendered impassable.

A good path runs to the right, south-east over an undulating spur

24

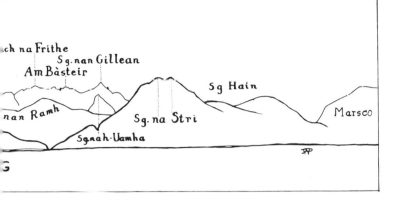

Ach na Frithe
Sg. nan Gillean
Am Bàsteir
Sg Hain
nan Ramh
Sg. na Stri
Marsco
Sgnah-Uamha

back to the shore of Loch Scavaig. Ahead huge slabs, constituting the west face of Sgùrr na Stri, gradually encroach to the edge of the sea. Here at the Bad Step (formerly known as Ceum Carach - Ladies' Step) the gabbro curves over into the waves.

'Salvation' has misguidedly been afforded by the Army. Explosives have been employed to provide a 'route' 200 feet above the sea. This seems very exposed and a slip here would mean curtains, or a wetting. However, unless the sea is rough it is simpler, less tiring and quicker to take the short scramble along a shelf then a crack-cum-gangway traversing a sloping slab some 15 feet above salt-water. Now a step down lands one on a pavement overhung by rocks. This 'cave' feature provides the starting point on the northward journey when the route is less obvious. Remember not to go too high. Cross the overhung platform to the left then make a move left and up onto a crack rising across, then petering out on the huge slab. Half-way along the crack a shelf goes off to the left to a wider one taking you to vegetation again. The path rounding the southern slopes of Sgùrr na Stri is straightforward. The sea-scape changes as the headlands of Rubha Buidhe and Rubha Bàn (8 miles 3 furlongs) are passed. The army's efforts are evident again. Their suspension foot-bridge across the Camasunary River has survived and conducts one to the bothy, pasture and farm buildings of Camasunary (10 miles 2 furlongs).

The final leg to Elgol comprises a walk south above Scavaig Bay. In

25

one mile the path climbs above shaly sea cliffs then descends to cross the bottom of Glen Scaladal. Finally a rising traverse of the steep shale and sandstone face of Ben Cleat brings the path to the scattered crofts of Elgol, 3 miles 2 furlongs from Camasunary, 6 miles from Coruisk.

The Bad Step may be completely avoided by a safe but tiring alternative involving good navigation along the route, Coruisk-Loch Coire Riabhaich - col between Sgùrrs Na Stri and Hain - west bank of Abhainn Camas Fhionnairigh (Camasunary River) - Suspension Bridge.

The emergency 'Walk-Out' from Camasunary should be over the Màm to Kirkibost, *Route 3*.

Coruisk is a serious place to evacuate other than by boat. The most direct route to civilisation is Bealach Coire na Banachdich, *(Route 10)* 6¼ miles of rough walking over a difficult pass.

The Passes

		Metres	Feet	Grade
Route 5	BEALACH A' GARBH-COIRE	797	2,614	3S
Route 6	BEALACH COIRE' AN LOCHAIN	855	2,806	3S
Route 7	BEALACH COIR' A' GHRUNNDA*	841	2,759	2W
Route 8	BEALACH SGUMAIN*	921	3,023	3S
Route 9	BEALACH MHIC COINNICH	892	2,928	3S
Route 10	BEALACH COIRE NA BANACHDICH	851	2,791	2W
Route 11	AN DORUS	847	2,779	3S
Route 12	BEALACH NA GLAIC MOIRE	760	2,492	2W
Route 13	'BEALACH HARTA'	760	2,494	2W
Route 14	BEALACH NAN LICE	896	2,940	2W
Route 15	BEALACH A' BHASTEIR	833	2,733	2W
Route 16	BEALACH A' GHLAS-CHOIRE	640	2,099	2W

*Pass on Lateral Ridge only i.e. not on Main Ridge

Routes 5-16 constitute all the ways taken across the Main Ridge which involve no more than simple scrambling, though in one or two cases route finding is none too obvious. Reaching a pass constitutes the greater part of most ascents of the peaks. Four of them provide alternate ways between Glen Brittle and Coruisk (5, 6, 9 and 10). Routes are described 'inwards' to the centre of the Cuillin from Glen Brittle or Sligachan.

5. BEALACH A' GARBH-CHOIRE 2,614ft.
Easy Scrambling/Rough Walking 3S
Glen Brittle 4 miles, Coruisk Hut 2 miles 7 furlongs
2,700 feet of ascent

From Glen Brittle follow Route 4 before the path skirting the boulder-strewn slopes of Sròn na Ciche descends towards the stream draining Coir' a' Ghrunnda (3 miles). Where the path crosses a glacis by a perched boulder a lesser track takes a rising traverse on the left beneath the smooth 600 feet high North and South Crags, that harbour many good climbs. Here a cairned route runs along a scree shelf avoiding the awkward, rounded, boiler-plate slabs in the bed of the corrie down on the right. A final band of slabs guarding the upper corrie is easily overcome 25 yards left of the stream. The loch beyond is the largest of the Cuillin's meagre collection of four. In sunshine its surface assumes a turquoise hue in contrast to the brown-gold cliffs and the intervening bouldery wastes and slopes.

Above the far shore of the Lochan the depression between Sgùrr Dubh na Da Bheinn, the peak rising straight from the water, and Sgùrr nan Eag over on the right, is graced by the square mass of Caisteal a' Garbh-choire. Pass either side of this rocky turret after a climb up big bouldery slopes. The easier pass to the south (4 miles) is 21 feet lower at 2,614 feet than its northern partner where a large rock bridges the gap.

An Garbh-choire, made like Coir' a' Ghrunnda of peridotite the coarsest of rocks, really *is* rough. The chaos of boulders below is best negotiated by sticking below the gabbro walls of the Dubh ridge on the left. After a mile, two ways take one to the Coruisk Hut.

(a)   Continue under cliffs avoiding rock bands extending towards the Mad Burn (Allt a' Chaoich) at 1200 feet and 900 feet altitude to reach the floor of Coruisk at a damp patch at the base of the slabs on the left. Rounding the south (right) of this wet area the shore path is encountered and followed to the right to the stepping stones at the outlet of Loch Coruisk. *(See Route 2)*.

(b)   In dry weather descend below the rock-bands and follow the Mad Burn to the right keeping on the south (right) bank. This route involves scrambling before the sea-shore of Loch Scavaig is attained. Half-way to the hut, slabs from Meall nan Cuilce reaching the sea must be crossed and may be awkward if slippery.
Glen Brittle - Coruisk Hut 6 miles 7 furlongs.

6.   BEALACH COIR' AN LOCHAIN   2,806 feet
Easy Scrambling/ Rough Walking 3S
Glen Brittle 4 miles, Coruisk Hut 3 miles
2,900 feet of ascent

Route 5 is taken to the Lochan in Coir' a' Ghrunnda at 2,290 feet.

Our pass is erroneously entitled the Thearlaich-Dubh Gap on the 6 inch maps. The pass does conduct you between Sgùrrs Thearlaich and Dubh na Da Bheinn. The 'Gap' is a deep, overhung rent in the rocky ridge 100 yards north of the Bealach proper. The 400 feet from the Lochan is easily taken if larger stones are used.

The descent from Bealach Coir' an Lochain to the pool in Coir' an Lochain involves a loss of 1,000 feet in altitude and lies half a mile to the north east. Here the scenery is untamed. Few climbers find their way to this corrie which if anything is even more difficult of access than Coir' a' Ghrunnda. The lochan's altitude is 1840 feet.

The burn issuing from the lochan eventually slides down hundreds of feet of steep slabs. A cairned route can be found by following the burn for 150-160 yards from the outlet. From here the line of cairns extends down and right (north east) for 250 yards to a terrace which slants down and right again between huge slabby tiers of gabbro finally emerging into Coir 'a' Chaoruinn. This 'corrie' is simply a tilted vegetated scoop amid the slabby 3,000 feet north east face of Sgùrr Dubh Mòr. The central watercourse draining this hollow finds the easiest way down a final short slab 200 feet above the upper, north west end of Loch Coruisk. Turn right along the path along the shore for its 1½ miles and join Route 2 at the stepping stones.
Glen Brittle to Coruisk Hut 7 miles.

7. BEALACH COIR' A' GHRUNNDA   2,759ft
Rough, Loose Walking   2W
Glen Brittle 2 miles 3 furlongs

This col lies between Sròn na Ciche and Sgùrr Sgumain and is a convenience name applied long ago to the head of the Sgumain Stone Shoot. The stone shoot provides a confident climber with one of the easiest descents to Coire Làgan from the surrounding heights. Although our pass lies on a lateral ridge it can be 'taken' en route to, or from Glen Brittle and any of the peaks south of Sgùrr Alasdair providing a more direct alternative to the tricky slabs in Coir' a' Ghrunnda.

From the Memorial Hut walk 50 yards down the road towards Glen Brittle House, turn left before the stone pens and follow a path for 300 yards then cross the burn on stones just downstream of Glen Brittle's water-intake. On the far side a path is joined which follows the south bank of the stream through the wooded 'garden' at the back of the house. After a steep rise the well-worn track fetches one to the rim of a deep cauldron. Across the far side of this hollow our stream effects a single leap into the basin. This is Eas Mór, one of Scotland's spectacular falls. The peaks of Banachdich and Dearg provide a deserving backcloth to the scene. Instead of following the burn one adopts the much-used peaty track across the boggy moor taking one south-east. Loch an Fhir-bhaillaich lies in a shallow depression 50 yards to the right. Before one comes opposite its far end the track divides and the right-hand fork is followed crossing yet another track running directly from the camp site onto the north bank of Coire Làgan. Our route maintains altitude but crosses the main burn to the base of the huge 1,000 feet high ½ mile long precipice of Sròn na Ciche. Here is the most popular climbing crag in the Cuillin. Looking left or east along the base of the cliff a scree-filled depression is seen dividing Sròn na Ciche from the buttress of Sgùrr Sgumain seen 'end-on'. The narrow right-hand branch rising away from us is the Sgumain Stone-shoot.

The 1,000 feet ascent is steep and loose and passes the Ladies' Pinnacle on the left. This was first climbed by Mrs Colin Philip and Miss Prothero and gives an optional scramble and care must be made on the short 30 feet climb from the narrow neck behind the top. A little way above this the col is reached.

On the Ghrunnda side the rock is peridotite. Continue east and slant down a boulder shoot to the left to reach the north end of the loch in Coir' a' Ghrunnda within a quarter mile with a loss of 450 feet in height. In a hollow over half way down, lies a house-sized boulder resting on smaller ones, follow the left (east) bank of a stream to a peculiar mossy flat where it enters the lochan.

8. BEALACH SGUMAIN 3,023ft.
Steep Loose Walking on scree 2W/3S

Glen Brittle 2 miles 5 furlongs,
Loch Coir' a Ghrunnda 2 furlongs

Probably this pass will not be used. You may visit the Bealach while crossing between Sgùrr Sgumain and Sgùrr Alasdair. It is hoped you have no cause to climb the interminable, exceedingly loose and frighteningly steep scree above Coire Làgan to this, the highest bealach on Skye. Consult the next route (9) for the walk to the loch in Coire Làgan, 2 miles 3 furlongs. A hundred yards upstream, face right and you are in a direct line with the scree-run from the Great Stone Shoot which descends the couloir between the gully-seamed wall of Sgùrr Thearlaich (left) and the basalt North face or ridge of Sgùrr Alasdair. 600 feet up the Stone Shoot a break on the right above a line of rock takes you under Alasdair's steep nose. Finally a way goes up over very steep scree to the col which boasts a few pinnacles.

The 700 feet descent to the loch in Coir' a' Ghrunnda can be made more or less directly from a point a little way up the Alasdair ridge, again on scree which however is not as steep as that on the north side.

9. BEALACH MHIC CHOINNICH 2,928ft.
Steep Scree and Scrambling 3S

Glen Brittle 2 miles 5 furlongs, Coruisk hut 4 miles

Coire Làgan is enclosed by the highest and most dominant summits of the Cuillin. Strangely a simple scree slope leads from the basin to each gap between each of these peaks. Only one of these, however conducts the walker *across* the Main Ridge to Coruisk. This important pass, conveniently adopting the name of the peak immediately to its north, is nevertheless a high one and requires a little scrambling.

From Glen Brittle take Route 7 as far as Loch an Fhir-Bhallaich (1 mile 3 furlongs). Follow the left-hand path at the fork above the loch. The path climbs gradually avoiding slabby rocks by the stream to Loch Làgan at 1860 feet (2 miles 3 furlongs). All around soaring basaltic peaks frown on a tiny oasis of grass fringing the small but delightful pool. Here a tent could be pitched and a superb base established amidst the most celebrated climbing in Skye.

The Great Stone Shoot between Sgùrrs Alasdair and Thearlaich is in line with a point 120 yards upstream from the lochan. Although the objective, Bealach Mhic Coinnich, lies left of Thearlaich below the steep southern face of Sgùrr Mhic Coinnich, start right of the Stone Shoot and hug the lowest rocks of Sgùrr Alasdair. This manoeuvre avoids large and unstable block-scree. 700 feet above the lochan the rock walls of both Thearlaich and Alasdair close in. Cross the Stone Shoot and continue left above the screes into the couloir falling from the bealach. The left side contains the best approach, a little simple scrambling being encountered just below the top of the pass.

Steep and difficult rock walls guard the mountains on either hand but ahead and down there is no difficulty apart from two 6 feet steps in corners against the Mhic Coinnich side.   Scree or boulders are encountered on the descent into Coireachan Ruadha or Coir' an Lochain, left and right respectively of an indeterminate ridge falling from the north end of Sgùrr Thearlaich and linking with Sgùrr Coir' an Lochain.

(a)   To reach the head of Coir' Uisg bear N.E. and skirt the base of the crags of the west face of Sgùrr Coir' an Lochain onto open slopes leading down to a burn flowing in from the left. Paths accompany the watercourse to the head of Loch Coruisk and then along its shore to the Coruisk Hut (6 miles 5 furlongs from Glen Brittle).

(b)   Alternatively 200 feet below the bealach trend right and cross the Thearlaich-Sgúrr Coir 'an Lochain 'ridge' and descend, trending right to pick up a stream flowing into the lochan of Coir' an Lochain 1,840 feet. Hence Route 6 takes you down to the Coruisk Hut via Coir' a' Chaoruinn (5 miles 6 furlongs from Glen Brittle).

10.   BEALACH COIRE NA BANACHDICH   2,791ft.
Rough Walking   2W

Glen Brittle 2 miles 2 furlongs, Coruisk Hut 4 miles

If the correct route is found on its western approach this pass affords the easiest and most direct route between Glen Brittle and Coruisk. Commence this crossing by following one of the paths described in Route 7 to Eas Mor. Skirt the edge of the hollow (*do not* fall into one of the steep rifts extending across the peaty track here and there) and follow the trail hugging the precipitous south bank of the main burn of Coire na Banachdich. Before a second ravine a mile out of Glen Brittle the O.S. map shows the path continuing on the opposite bank. We will stay on the south bank and follow a more direct path up the rough but open hollow. The castellated Window Buttress stands to our right. Its remarkable tower, pierced by two 'windows' is a feature of the view from the windows of the Memorial Hut, especially when mist lying in the upper hollow demonstrates that a rocky tower lies on the steep northern flank of Sgùrr Dearg. Here lies the nearest rock-climbing to Glen Brittle. Directly beneath the Window Tower the path crosses a tributary draining a rocky amphitheatre high on the right. Between this crossing and the pass the Banachdich Gully falls directly. Unless you are prepared to emulate the efforts of Messrs. Gibbs, King and MacKenzie in 1898 who overcame the four vertical pitches in the rift, one at least graded 'Difficult' by climbers, your way is a track marked by cairns and goes

32

off half right, when the floor steepens, up a shallow gully right of some slabs, right of the gully. Broken ground then a well-cairned scree shoot beneath the crags of Sgùrr Dearg on the right, leads to a broad, shelving terrace. The terrace leads left over scree to the summit of the bealach. An extra 'dog-leg' shown on the O.S. map should be ignored.

When descending to Glen Brittle, a surer way from the pass could be made via Route 48 to the summit of Sgùrr Dearg and descending Route 47 West Ridge. The extra 500 feet of ascent is compensated for by more gradual gradients on the descent to the valley.

The bealach marked by a rock 'lump' is impressive. The North Face of Sgùrr Dearg is very spectacular and harbours some of the hardest rock-climbs in Skye on its dark overhangs. The screes descending to Coireachan Ruadha are not too steep but are loose enough to warrant a diversion to the base of the gigantic wall on the Dearg side to gain a surer footing during an ascent of the pass. On the left (N) the lower buttress or nose of Sròn Bhuidhe is composed or rather de-composed of reddish Peridotite whose detritus in these parts gives Coireachan Ruadha its name.

The rest of the descent to Coir' Uisg is simple enough, suffice to mention some slabby rocks at 1600 feet which are avoided on the right before continuing alongside the burn to join the path along the shore of Loch Coruisk to the hut on Loch Scavaig.

11. AN DORUS   2,779ft.
Scree Walking/Awkward Scrambling on East Side   3S
Glen Brittle 2 miles 5 furlongs, Coruisk Hut 4 miles

'The Door' is a historically important pass. Apparently the Clan McLeod used it during their 'military activities' in the days of yore. A deep and narrower gap about half-way up the connecting ridge of Sgùrr a' Ghreadaidh to the south, known as Eag Dubh is confused with our pass on some maps. The Coruisk side of An Dorus must be reserved for seasoned scramblers. The western approach which begins at the youth hostel in Glen Brittle is easy and straightforward. A path follows the true left i.e. south bank of a large stream that flows past the hostel. This burn, the Allt a'Choire Ghreadaidh runs through some lovely ravines. On a hot day a more tempting method of keeping cool than exuding buckets of perspiration on the screes and slabs of the surrounding hills is provided here. Half a mile beyond the last ravine a reedy hollow marks the end of the path but you continue over sparse vegetation along

33

the burn until it forks under the gullied and shadowed face of An Diallaid. The upper corries are divided by the rocky N.W. spur of Sgùrr a' Ghreadaidh. The north branch is favoured by the title Coire na Dorus which patently is that which is taken to put one's foot in the door, so to speak. The scree-run falling from the summit of the pass is 800 feet in vertical height and ends just left of the lowest rocks of the 'N.W. spur' - Sgùrr Eadar Da Choire.

The descent into Coir' an Uaigneis comprises the narrow An Dorus Gully. The gully is mainly scree but a few rock slopes require careful negotiation. After scrambling down 200 feet, open scree slopes lead to a more stable terrain. 800 feet of direct descent brings one to a more level hollow graced by some small pools. Under them precipitous rocks boasting 800 feet severe rock climbs bar access to Coir'-Uisg. On the north side of the shelf, left of the pools, a small stream flows down a rock defile. Left or north of this again a safe way down will be found alongside the defile. Beyond a further stream on the left will be found the path from Bealach na Glaic Moire (Route 12) to the Coruisk Hut.

12. BEALACH NA GLAIC MOIRE   2,492ft.
Rough Walking - Complicated   2W

Glen Brittle (Road) 2 miles 6 furlongs.
Sligachan 5½ miles,
Coruisk Hut 3 miles 7 furlongs

This the lowest pass on the Main Ridge has three approaches. The paths are fairly well marked. The bealach is especially useful as a highway between Sligachan and upper Coir' Uisg.

(a)   The natural approach comes from the West. Vergeside parking is possible along the road north from Glen Brittle above the confluence of Allt an Fhamhair and the Brittle River, a little over two miles from the youth hostel. A path begins just downstream of the stream junction and follows the true right or north bank of the Brittle. A large boulder is passed before encountering the Allt a' Mhaim. A stride takes one over this stream and we continue following the main burn now named after Coir' a' Mhadaidh. Spectacular rock basins, The Fairy Pools where an underwater rock arch spans turquoise deeps. These waters provide local relief in the moorland scene before we cross yet another stream flowing in from the left draining the 'Corrie of the Thunderer'. We stand in the centre of Coire na Creiche, a vast bowl of moorland, boulders and

34

slabs, hemmed in by a two-mile wall of crags between 400 and 1,400 feet high. Dominating this scene is the shapely rock-cone of Sgùrr an Fheadain which projects well out into the corrie, its lowest slabs falling as low as the 1,000 feet contour. The higher reaches at either hand of the peak are named Coire' a' Tarneilear on the left or north and Coir' a' Mhadaidh to the south. On maps published prior to 1965 these names were printed conversely and to prevent confusion climbing guides conformed to this error. At last the Ordnance Survey has re-named them and guidebooks now place Coir' a' Mhadaidh below the peak of the same name.

Choosing the driest route continue along the burn to Coir' a' Mhadaidh. When the floor of the basin steepens a vague track terracing in from the right, is met (1 mile 7 furlongs) beneath the first rock outcrops. This cairned track originates on the Bealach a' Mhaim and this constitutes a long but easy approach from Sligachan *(see Route 1).*

(b)   Leave Route 1 from Sligachan just beyond the summit of the path, and take up a track crossing the infant stream above the pool and then ascend slightly across the base of Sròn Tobar nan Uaislean, the ridge rising on the left. Traverse the mile-wide slope of Bruach na Frithe 200 feet below the lowest rock bands to cross the burn draining Coir' a' Tarneilear at the 800 feet contour 200 feet below the Slabs of Sgùrr an Fheadain. Beyond the stream the track rises to join our route from Glen Brittle (1 mile 5 furlongs from Bealach a' Mhaim).

The burn from Coir' a' Mhadaidh above this point falls pleasantly between rocks, and if one adopts this route some scrambling is involved which may be impossible in wet conditions. A cairned way on the left is available up a square sided gully onto bouldery terrain. A high band of slabs now prevents direct access to our pass lying immediately above. The South Gully in line with the stream is graded 'Severe' and was not climbed until 1937! This gully constitutes the natural division between the difficult peaks of Sgùrr a' Mhadaidh and Bidein Druim nan Ramh (on the left). To reach our pass we encroach on the latter mountain. The next break in the slabs (going left) is another deep cut gully, the Central (difficult); a further 100 yards is the last, North Gully (moderate), before a loose scree-run narrow at first provides a continuous and safe 800 feet climb to a wide ledge. From the base of the scree-run, another easy route on the left leads north–north-east between rocks to the saddle behind the summit rocks of Sgùrr an Fheadain. From the top of the scree-run, easy slopes on the left can be crossed under the north-west face of Bidein to reach 'Bealach Harta' *(Route 13)*. We however, can now turn right above the slabs to reach the top of our pass. An alternative worth mentioning is the approach up Allt Coir' a' Tarneilear ending with a traverse below Bidein's peaks to the easy continuation south along the Main Ridge to the Bealach.

400 feet down the Coir' Uisg side a rocky rib divides the Glac Mhór in two. The screes in the south branch are more stable and from them one of the highest springs on the island issues - recommendation enough! Rejoining the other branch, a further 500 feet below, a path leads down into the oasis of Coir' Uisg. Where the waters from Coireachan Ruadha are reached on the valley floor, paths take to the northern and southern shores of Loch Coruisk. If streams are in spate adopt whichever side of the river/loch you require *now*.

If Camusunary is your objective the correct bank is the *left* one, which in a mile takes one by the braided stream to the loch. The way beneath a steep buttress and huge slabs is rough. An indefinite path crosses the Allt a' Choire Riabhaich before the track from Sligachan is joined *(Route 2)*. Camasunary from Glen Brittle is 9½ miles. Elgol is 12½ miles with 2,400 feet of climbing compared with 13½ miles and 2,000 feet via the 'Shore Path' *(Route 4)*.

(d)   The route to the Coruisk Hut from the head of Coir' Uisg of course leads down the right or south bank of the river and follows the southern shore of the loch to the hut. Distances from Glen Brittle 6 miles 5 furlongs and Sligachan 9 miles 3 furlongs. Sligachan to Coruisk *(Route 2)* with difficult river crossing 7 miles 3 furlongs with 1,400 feet of ascent.

13.   'BEALACH HARTA'   2,494ft.
Easy but Rough   2W

Sligachan 6 miles 5 furlongs, Glen Brittle 2 miles 6 furlongs

Significantly this pass has received scant recognition from previous guide books. It provides the only easy route between the important valleys of Glen Brittle and Harta Corrie. Further it is the second lowest point on the Main Ridge - scarcely two feet higher than Bealach na Glaic Moire! Though the crossing to be described is rough it is direct and worthy of baptism. Until a more authoritative suggestion is made this guide will for convenience entitle the pass - Bealach Harta. Its importance as an approach to the Ridge from Sligachan is slight as Route 12 provides a long but rapid descent to the hotel along good-ish paths. Anyone using Harta Corrie as a base will find the pass a useful one, so the crossing is described from east to west.

From Sligachan follow Route 2 to Lochan Dubha (3½ miles). Before the path comes opposite the first of the twin sheets of water a vague track runs west (right) and brings you alongside the Sligachan River. The south bank is followed upstream for a mile to the gigantic Bloody Stone (4¾ miles). This monolith gives useful shelter. It is named from an action in which some McLeods were massacred by the MacDonalds. Nowadays all is peace and quiet except for the gusting of the wind and the flow of the river when in spate. Continue up the valley with easy slopes on the left leading south over Meall an Dearg. Gradually the wide and shallow waters flow beneath the shapely cone of Sgùrr na h-Uamha, the terminus of the Main Ridge proper. A mile and a half beyond the Bloody Stone the main stream flows past some small crags on the right. Left of, and beyond these a wide stony break divides the high slabs forming the western wall of Harta Corrie in which we are now ensconsed.

The 1,500 feet ascent of the hollow goes between the slabs of An Caisteal and the more broken face of Bidein Druim nan Ramh and follows the lowest rocks of the latter but trending if anything to the right where in doubt, finally passing on scree just right of the summit buttresses of Bidein. The easiest scree run reaches the Main Ridge 30 yards south-east of the lowest point. To descend to Coir' a' Tarneilear turn right and follow the ridge for sixty yards to a rock wall across the ridge. Go north from here over loose slopes and avoiding rocky bluffs by moving left until in line with a continuous scree-run dropping steeply to a hollow of grass and boulders. Two streams develop here. The left-hand has cut a ravine. The right (N.E.) bank of the right-hand stream is easy to follow across another hollow, then down across slopes of slabby rock and scree well above the stream along a developing track. This eventually crosses back to the left bank of the stream after it passes the lowest bluffs of Sgùrr an Fhèadain. Hereabouts the path from Sligachan and the Mam crosses the stream and traverses the broken heather slopes for Bealach na Glaic Moire *(Route 12)*. Recross the Allt Coir' a'

Tarneilear, follow the right (N) bank again until a path develops leading past the picturesque rock-pools. Cross the Allt a' Mhaim stream then gradually ascend the boggy slopes and make a final stream crossing on the Mam (*Route 1*) path a few yards below a forest fence and 100 yards short of the Glen Brittle road.

14. BEALACH NAN LICE   2940ft

N. approach Easy, S. approach not obvious   2W
Sligachan 4¼ miles, Bealach a' Mhaim 1¾ miles

Formerly known as Bealach a' Leitir, this high saddle is rarely used as a pass. Rain falling at either side eventually finds its way beneath the bridges at Sligachan. As an approach to the northern peaks from Fionn or Lota Corries it might prove useful. The southern approach is much less straight forward than the northern and will therefore be described in ascent.

Adopt Route 13 and continue alongside the main stream, feeding Sligachan River. Access to Lota Corrie, a higher shelf above the parent Harta Corrie, is barred by a continuous amphitheatre of rock, not very high, down which the head waters of the Sligachan River fall and slide. 200 yards right, east of the fall, bouldery slopes turn the obstacle. Regain the stream just above the fall. A loss of 200 feet in height is incurred. The main stream is followed just left of a bluff immediately beyond the fall until the ground begins to steepen. One now heads N.W. along the left-hand of two branch streams to a stone shoot continuing down in the same line between Sgùrr a' Fionn Choire, the slabby stepped rock peak to the left and the tortured precipices of Am Basteir and his 'Tooth' to the right. Just before the top of the pass a detached 20 feet pinnacle near the right wall of the stone shoot forms a landmark. (7½ miles from Sligachan).

Returning to the top of the waterfall a more westerly course can bring you to a rockier scree slope leading below the south-west wall of Sgùrr a' Fionn Choire to a higher saddle 2,964 feet which also gives a way across the ridge. It should be noted that Bealach a' Bhasteir can also be reached from Lota Corrie (*see Route 15*).

From the top of our pass Coire a' Bhàsteir can be gained by rounding the low rock ridge leading east and following the base of its north wall under the Bàsteir Tooth then descending scree. For Fionn Choire which Bealach nan Lice properly serves, one simply continues straight down on a north-westerly cairned route down the bowl of scree. The floor of the Fionn Choire makes for very comfortable walking, a change for the Cuillin, as a course down this open valley can be made on short grass. If the westerly slopes are used a line of cairns, rather widely spaced, descending from the ridge on the left might be picked up. On the open slopes below the corrie a path develops 100 yards west of and parallel to, the Allt an Fhionn Choire. It soon leads down to the Red Burn, crosses it, then follows the left bank. 200 yards downstream our track joins the main Bealach a' Mhaim path (*Route 1*).

15. BEALACH A' BHASTEIR 2733ft.

Rough Walking/Complicated   2W

Sligachan 31/4 miles (7 miles 1 furlong via Harta Corrie)

A well-used but high pass, though only the north flank carries any traffic. This approach is therefore described. The main road goes through a shallow cutting just west of the hotel. From the top of this bank a path undulates over heather to a corrugated shed, an old power house standing above the Red Burn. 70 yards upstream a footbridge gives access to the peat-covered moor stretching south for over a mile. A path meanders over this boggy waste taking advantage of old moraines to gain drier ground. At 1 3/4 miles the Little Red Burn is met and following its west bank the going becomes a little drier. 250 yards upstream a footbridge gives access to the famous 'Tourist Route' to Sgùrr nan Gillean, the Cuillin's most popular mountain. (2 miles) We stay on the right (west) bank of our stream and follow it crossing from basalt to gabbro at the 800 feet level. In the open valley above here, the path is less distinct but basically you continue on the right (west) side of the stream until rock walls curve in on either hand, marking the lower entrance to the dark and difficult depths of the Bhasteir Gorge. There is no need to emulate the naked exploits of the Alpine Club during the first journey up the ravine in 1890 however, as a cairned route climbs easily to a series of ledges leading up and across the slabs dipping over into the gorge. The cairns take you a couple of hundred feet above the gorge and run 100 yards to its right (facing up). A 400 feet climb brings you pleasantly into Coire a' Bhàsteir. The small lochan (2 miles 7 furlongs) is a resting place.

In spite of our having attained nigh on 2,000 feet, Sgùrr nan Gillean towers above this rock hollow graced by its tiny sheet of water. (Water bottles should be replenished here.) Gillean boasts a lower crag on this face, slit by two gullies. A trodden way across broken scree reaches the loose screes takes you beneath the bulging north face of the 'Executioner'. Follow the base of his oppressive cliffs to the left to reach Bealach a' Bhàsteir. Going right (west) instead brings one below the Tooth to Bealach nan Lice. 3 miles 3 furlongs.

From Bealach a' Bhasteir, a return to Sligachan can be made by descending southwards to a stream 900 feet below and following Route 14 to by-pass the waterfall and reach Lota Corrie.

The initial section is however an unpleasant if not disconcertingly steep zone of loose, brittle rock.

16. BEALACH A' GHLAS-CHOIRE 2,099ft.
Rough Walking   2W

Sligachan 5 miles. Via Harta Corrie 5 miles 5 furlongs

Bealach a' Beach was an alternative title for this pass. An integral crossing will rarely be made. Expeditions to this part of the Cuillin can more conveniently start or end by continuing north along the ridge and descending Sgùrr nan Gillean's Tourist Path *(Route 86)*.

After Route 14 turns the waterfall above Harta Corrie, one is faced on the right by a simple but steep walk directly upwards for 500 feet to the bealach.

The eastern approach can involve a trackless boggy stumble if the western bank of the Sligachan River is followed. If the river is low, use Route 14 then ford it south to north between Lochan Dubha and the Bloody Stone, then Allt a' Ghlais-choire or the adjacent slope to the south can be ascended directly to the top of the pass.

The Peaks

SGÙRR NAN EAG GROUP

GARS-BHEINN 2,935ft.

Route 17	Coir' a' Chruidh	Ascended from Coruisk	2W
Route 18	Coire Beag	Coruisk	2W
Route 19	East Ridge	Glen Brittle/Coruisk	2W
Route 20	South West Flank	Glen Brittle	2W
Route 21	Ridge to Sgùrr a' Choire Bhig		1W

SGÙRR A' CHOIRE BHIG 2872ft.

Route 21	Ridge from Gars-bheinn	2W
Route 22	From Sgùrr nan Eag	2W

41

SGÙRR NAN EAG 3031ft.

Route 22	Ridge to Sgùrr a' Choire Bhig		2W
Route 23	South-West Flank	Glen Brittle	2W
Route 24	North-West Ridge	Glen Brittle/Coruisk	3S

The southern chain of the Cuillin provides the easiest section of the Main Ridge Traverse and yet no simple and direct crossing can be made hereabouts. The only recommended rock climbs which could be useful to that aim are the North-East Ridges of Sgùrr a' Choire Bhig and Gars-bheinn which are graded moderate and easy respectively. The slabs defending the head of the open Coire nan Laogh west of the ridge are cut by three neglected gullies. The West (Moderate), the Central (Very Difficult) and the East (Difficult) provide routes for the climber.

The crest of the ridge with the exception of the top of Sgùrr a' Choire Bhig is gabbro. This and the lower flanks of the western side, the North East Ridge of Gars-bheinn and the Coir' a' Chruidh are basalt, and An Garbh-choire is peridotite.

GARS-BHEINN 2,935ft.

A famed view point, this the southernmost peak of the Cuillin, dominates the sea and affords an uninterrupted maritime panorama embracing the Western Highlands, the Small Isles (Rhum is particularly in evidence) to the south, and the Outer Hebrides just visible on the far western horizon. The summit is a substantial though neat affair. Several ledges provide resting places. In mist it is worth noting that two minor rocky tops lie to the west. Between them and the parent summit two scree shoots lead down into Coire Beag on the north, uniting 2-300 feet below the Main Ridge.

Descents. In mist the only safe way off the mountain is to take the South West Flank Route 20 and join Route 4 which should be clear of any mountain cloud. Even so care should be taken not to cross and miss the sketchy track crossing the moor.

17. GARS-BHEINN VIA COIR' A' CHRUIDH 2W
Coruisk 2 miles 3,000ft of ascent

The only approaches from the Coruisk side for the walker are

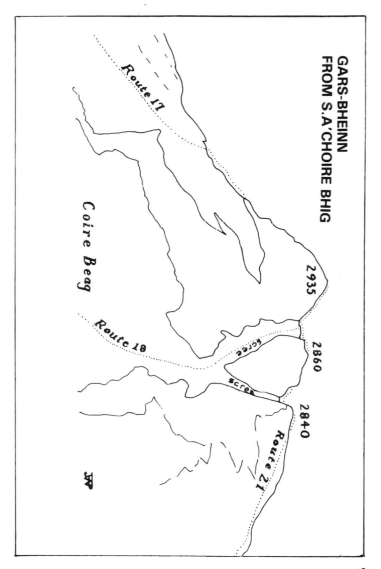

GARS-BHEINN
FROM S.A'CHOIRE BHIG

Route 11

Coire Beag

Route 18

2935

scree

2860

scree

2840

Route 21

SP

through Coire Beag and Coir' a' Chruidh. Route 4 is reversed from the hut as far as Allt Coir' a' Chruidh (7 furlongs). Hence one heads uphill towards Gars-bheinn until the wall of the north-east ridge confronts one. Now lead to the left below the wall to a minor rise on the main ridge some 200 yards south-east of the summit.

18. GARS-BHEINN VIA COIRE BEAG   2W/R1
Coruisk 1¾ miles   3,000ft of ascent

Reverse Route 5 to the junction of the Mad Burn with the streams which drain An Garbh-choire and Coire Beag. The eastern tributary from the latter corrie is followed. A narrow shelf on the right leads into the upper sanctuary, 500 yards beyond the upper rocks of the **Mad Burn Buttress** and above a line of cliffs passed on the right. Rock-climbers will prefer to take the more interesting but 'greasy' North-East Ridge on the left of the shelf. It is graded 'Easy. We continue up the upper corrie to a scree-filled gully leading up and left to a head wall. Ignore the branch climbing right and emerge onto the Main Ridge at a dip between a subsidiary top and the summit which lies close at hand on the left up simple rocks.

19. GARS-BHEINN EAST RIDGE   2W
Coruisk 2¼ miles   3,000ft of ascent

Those using Coruisk as a base for traversing the Main Ridge make the usual approach. Route 4 is reversed to the Allt na Fraoich (1 mile 5 furlongs). This stream is followed to a hollow, higher up, which sports a small pool. Broken, easy ground leads north for 500 yards to another hollow. A shorter way to this point can be seen on the map. The conical eastern terminus of Gars-bheinn now rears above, consisting of scree. The way lies directly over this to the start of the ridge at 2,200 feet (1¼ miles). Beyond, the ridge provides easier going right to the summit, with the crags of Coire a' Chruidh dropping pleasantly on the right with scree-slopes falling in the opposite direction to the Sound of Soay.

20. GARS-BHEINN SOUTH FLANK   2W
Glen Brittle House 4¾ miles   3,100ft of ascent

Most climbers use Glen Brittle as a base these days and this route provides the simplest means of attaining the summit of the Cuillin for the usual south-north traverse. (This is a good route to recommend to unfriendly rivals. A friend once met 'a man who died on it')

From the campsite use Route 4 and cross the burn draining Coire nan Laogh (3 miles 7 furlongs). Turn uphill over grass veering right whenever you feel like it. After a quarter mile the ground steepens and you shortly reach the loose and infuriating screes over which the last 1,600 feet are taken. A rock-band could be encountered but it is not continuous and a way through will be found without any great detour. In mist the summit ridge might be attained left or right of the top. Therefore note that two minor summits lie just west of the neat summit cairn.

SGÙRR A' CHOIRE BHIG 2,872ft.

Little more than a large top along a narrow ridge, this peak which was named in the 1890's by Collie or Naismith sends down a turretted ridge into An Garbh-choire which rock-climbers grade 'Moderate' and deem worthwhile. From the summit (a good view-point for the 'Dubhs') this drops away inconspicuously.

Descents. Whether visibility is good or bad, go south along the main ridge to the four tops of Gars-bheinn. For Glen Brittle turn right (south-west) at the first top and descend straight down the scree watching for the odd cliff to rejoin Route 4. For Coruisk, Route 19 is probably safest.

21. SGÙRR A'CHOIRE BHIG FROM GARS-BHEINN (EAST RIDGE) 2W

Glen Brittle 5 miles 3 furlongs, 3,300ft of ascent
Coruisk 2 miles 7 furlongs, 3,100ft of ascent

Once embarked on this expedition the walker must continue on the ridge (*Route 22)* at least until Bealach a' Garbh-choire (*Route 5)* is reached, beyond the next peak, Sgùrr Eag. From Gars-bheinn leave the cairn with the steepest ground on the right and head west to the top of the stone-shoot leading down to Coire Beag. Cross a subsidiary top beyond to another dip with a second scree-shoot descending north. Beyond a second top (2,840) the ridge is flanked by rock walls and provides an exhilarating walk. The lowest point 2,740 feet is reached in a quarter mile. The 150 feet ascent to the top is short, only 5 furlongs beyond Gars-bheinn.

22. SGÙRR A'CHOIRE BHIG FROM SGÙRR NAN EAG (WEST RIDGE)   2W

Glen Brittle 4½ miles, 3,400ft of ascent
Coruisk 4 miles, 3,300ft of ascent

Between these peaks no escape is possible. The walker must either return to Bealach a'Garbh-choire (*Route 5*) or continue to Gars-Bheinn *(Route 21)*. Nevertheless, it is a simple walk of similar character to that route.

The descent from Sgùrr nan Eag is straight-forward, to the dip at 2,537 feet (quarter mile). (Do not be tempted to leave the ridge, a way *can* be found into An Garbh-choire by traversing below the overhangs of Sgùrr nan Eag and the huge Chasm). On the ascent of Sgùrr a'Choire Bhig any difficulties can be avoided on the right or west.

SGÙRR NAN EAG   3,031ft.

The topography of the most southerly 'Munro' is simple. The central one of three faces on the south-west side of the Main Ridge is composed of infuriating scree plus an abundance of boulders. This face supports a virtually level ridge which maintains an altitude of 3,000 feet for a full quarter mile. On the west overlooking Coir' a' Ghrunnda is a loose cliff boasting a rock climb - West Buttress graded 'Difficult'. Right or south of the scree face a concave curtain of slabs stretches for ¾ mile around the head of Coire nan Laogh. On the Coruisk side of the ridge overhanging rocks abound and no choice of route exists for any but the advanced rock-climber. East of the summit a huge rift splits the mountain after which it is named:- The Chasm, 'Very Difficult'.

The summit cannot be much higher than several points along its straight and level roof. The topmost cairn is sited at the south-east end of the ridge.

Descents.   For Glen Brittle use the loose south-west flank, (*Route 23*). Beware of small outcrops after losing 800 feet. They are easily turned on the descent to the path on Route 4.

For Coruisk reverse Route 24 then Route 5.

Cnoc Leathan 560ft. It would be convenient here to mention Sgùrr Eag's tiny outlier south of the Shore Path. Approaches to this little-visited knoll are guarded by peat moss and marsh. The terraced appearance of the landscape is caused by the horizontal stratification of alternate layers of basalt and dolerite, reminiscent of Mull.

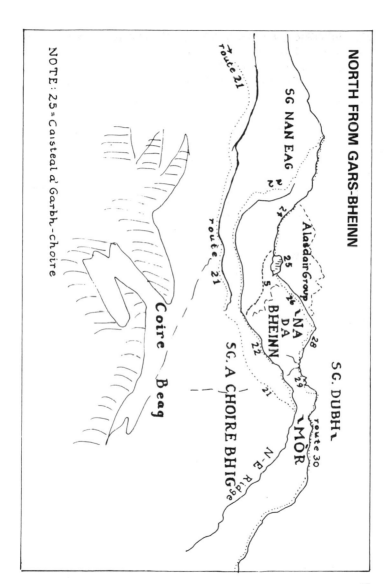

NORTH FROM GARS-BHEINN

NOTE : 25 = Caisteal a'Garbh-choire

route 21

SG NAN EAG

route 21

route 21

Coire Beag

Alasdair Group

25

5

NA DA BHEINN

26

28

22

29

21

SG. A CHOIRE BHIG

SG. DUBH

MÒR

route 30

N-E Ridge

23. SGÙRR NAN EAG — SOUTH-WEST FLANK 2W
Glen Brittle House 3 miles 7 furlongs   3,100ft of ascent

From Glen Brittle follow Route 4 to cross Allt Coir' a' Ghrunnda (3 miles). Leave the path and climb between outcrops going right when in doubt, to avoid shelves leading to impasses on the rockier face of the west side. Of the total 2,200 feet to climb above the path, the last 1,200 feet below the summit ridge is composed of loose scree and boulders. One has a wide area over which to pick one's way. One can always traverse right as the summit is found at the south-east end of the ridge.

24. SGÙRR NAN EAG — NORTH RIDGE 3S
Glen Brittle 4½ miles, 3,150ft of ascent
Coruisk 3 miles 3 furlongs, 3,050ft of ascent

After quitting Bealach a' Garbh-choire (Route 5 Glen Brittle 4 miles, Coruisk 2 miles 7 furlongs) a little rough scrambling will be encountered. The ridge is easy to follow and after two steep sections, levels out. The Summit Cairn lies at the far end of the level, narrow rock ridge, half a mile beyond and 500 feet higher than the Bealach.

THE DUBHS

CAISTEAL A' GARBH-CHOIRE   2,719ft.
Route 25   Traverse N-S   Glen Brittle/Coruisk   RII

SGÙRR DUBH NA DA BHEINN   3,078ft.
Route 26   S. Ridge   Glen Brittle/Coruisk   3S
Route 27   N.W. Ridge   Glen Brittle/Coruisk   3S
Route 28   E. Ridge   Coruisk   3S

SGÙRR DUBH MÒR   3096ft.
Route 29   S.W. Ridge   Coruisk   4S

SGÙRR DUBH BEAG   2,403ft.
Route 30   Traverse and E. Ridge of Dubh Mòr   Coruisk   RII

MEALL NA CUILCE   590ft.
Route 31   Ascent from Coruisk   IW - RIV

The most important of the lateral ridges of the Cuillin sends rocky slabs down to sea level. The traverse is one of the more delightful expeditions undertaken by roped parties staying at Coruisk, bare rock being under foot for two whole miles. Rough and lonely corries guard the approaches. The 1,000 feet south face is steep and rocky but so far no climbs have been recorded. The northern flanks only boast the famous descent by Nicolson and MacIntyre in 1874 and that, taken in darkness could not be described!

The 'Castle' and Sgùrr Dubh na Da Bheinn are peridotite, a coarser rock than the gabbro of which the remaining Dubhs are made. These peaks were named by the shepherds of the 19th century.

CAISTEAL A' GARBH-CHOIRE   2,719ft.

The peaklet stands athwart the pass of the same name. On a traverse of the Main Ridge, it can be turned on either side by a clamber over boulders and scree, sacrificing then regaining 200 feet in the process. 150 yards of rock walls separate the Bealach proper at 2,614ft from its northern twin at 2,635ft.

The best part of the view from the narrow summit is the lochan in Coir' a' Ghrunnda, backed by Sgumain, Alasdair and Thearlaich.

If one simply wishes to bag the top and return the easiest way, then use the south end with 2-300ft of easy climbing.

25. TRAVERSE OF CAISTEAL A' GARBH-CHOIRE
RII
Glen Brittle 4 miles, 2,850ft of ascent
Coruisk 2 miles 7 furlongs, 2,750ft of ascent.

Reach the Bealach a' Garbh-choire via Route 5. The traverse constitutes a moderate rock climb, short but enjoyable. The north end is very steep and difficult but is turned on the west. A difficult rock traverse *can* be made on the Ghrunnda side without gain or loss of height.

SGÙRR DUBH NA DA BHEINN 3,078ft

An undistinguished mountain, no rock climbing has been recorded on any of the three faces and ridges. The rocks are broken and the slopes have an abundance of scree. The north face is the steepest. None of the ridges provides any real difficulty, being well defined but not very narrow. The mountain is named because it lies at the junction of the Main and Dubhs ridges.

Some easy ground lies west of the summit whence the floors of corries Lochan, An Garbh and Ghrunnda are seen to advantage.

Descents. In mist reverse the south ridge to Route 5 and Coruisk. Glen Brittle is reached most safely via the North-West ridge and Route 6.

On a traverse, the summit may be avoided by a traverse between the cols across the loose, bouldery, west face, not recommended in mist.

26. SGÙRR DUBH NA DA BHEINN - SOUTH RIDGE
Glen Brittle 4¼ miles, 3,150ft of ascent   3S
Coruisk Hut 3 miles, 3,100ft of ascent

From the top of the north branch of Bealach a' Garbh-choire, where a large boulder perches on the ridge *(Route 5, 4 miles from Glen Brittle, 2 miles 7 furlongs from Coruisk)*, the south ridge has easy scrambling up some grooves and over boulders on its short 450ft climb. The top lies to the right of some open screes. A step is avoided on the left.

27. SGÙRR DUBH NA DA BHEINN - NORTH WEST RIDGE 3S

Glen Brittle 4¼ miles, 3,200ft of ascent
Coruisk 3¼ miles, 3,100ft of ascent

From Bealach Coir' an Lochain, 2,806ft *(Route 6)* a well defined ridge runs easily south east. Some rough scrambling is provided halfway with difficult steps avoided on the right, western side.

28. SGÙRR DUBH NA DA BHEINN - EAST RIDGE 3S

Coruisk 3 miles, an Garbh-choire 3¼ miles,
Coir' an Lochain. 3,100ft of ascent.

From Coruisk take Route 5 up An Garbh-choire until directly below Sgùrr Dubh Mòr. Immediately left of the rocks supporting the summit a steep and very rough boulder field leads to the high col between the peak and its brother to the west - Dubh na Da Bheinn. The col can also be reached by taking a more circuitous route via Route 6 to Coir' an Lochain. From the corrie another easy but chaotic jumble of boulders leads south, up to the col or dip at 2,907ft. From the col a short easy scramble leads west to the top. Easy going will be found to the left.

SGÙRR DUBH MÒR 3,096ft

This grand peak dominates a remote area of the Cuillin. The summit lies on the western extremity of a long ridge which appears as a level and massive wedge from other parts of the Cuillin.

Descents. The safest and simplest way off the topmost point is to take the steep south face. The way is scratched and provides good holds. Scree fields to the north seem to lead to holdless steps tantalisingly close to the boulder fields above Coir' an Lochain. Once off the top rocks of the peak, the way lies west round two blunt pinnacles to the gap before Sgùrr Dubh na Da Bheinn. For Coruisk, scree on the left (south), leads to An Garbh-choire and Route 5. For Glen Brittle use Route 28 to cross the summit of Sgùrr Dubh na Da Bheinn.

29. SGÙRR DUBH MÒR - WEST RIDGE 4S

Coruisk Hut, 3 miles, 3,100ft of ascent

Attain the dip at 2,907ft, west of the summit, via Routes 5 or 6 and

28. From here to the top of the highest Dubh is a difficult scramble. Three pinnacles are passed on the right before a steep, scratched section up rocks with good holds leads up the south face of the summit rocks. Sherrif Nicolson made the first ascent by this route on 6th September 1874.

SGÙRR DUBH BEAG 2,403ft

This peak is rarely visited for its own sake. The top can be reached from An Garbh-choire but the way is involved. The broad slabs to the east if taken by their easiest way, provide a pleasant easy rock climb RI. A rope may be required on a return journey.

Descents. One could reach Coruisk by descending the milder top section of the east ridge to a grassy rake cutting the line of descent at right angles at 1,580ft. The way down to the right seems clear of difficulty from below.

30. SGÙRR DUBH MOR, E. RIDGE and TRAVERSE OF SGÙRR DUBH BEAG   RII

Coruisk Hut 3 miles 3,100ft ascent to Sg. Dubh Mòr
Coruisk Hut 2½ miles 2,500ft ascent to Sg. Dubh Beag

From the hut follow the river and the south-west shore of the loch for 1¼ miles until one comes in line with the east corner of the massive ½ mile base of the overlapping ice-ground gabbro slabs. At 125 feet altitude one begins the easy rock-climb. The lowest overlap is overcome via a short grassy gully at the left end of the rocks. Thence easy angled slabs provide simple rock climbing punctuated by grassy platforms which serve to minimise any sense of exposure. After a broader ledge at 1,580 feet lies a rocky steeper section requiring the rope before a plateau makes progress easy as far as the summit of Sgùrr Dubh Beag.. To progress beyond this top go back and pass the top to the south (left) along a scree and grass terrace to reach the gap between. To obviate this move, the experienced mountaineer can effect an abseil over the overhang west of the top. Walking and bits of hand work prevail along the half mile narrower section of the ridge leading to the undulating summit ridge of the dominant peak. The topmost point lies at the farthest end.

31. MEALL NA CUILCE   590ft.   I W-RIV

This hill belongs to the Dubhs. Its summit is easy to visit from the

Mad Burn after that stream has been followed above the level of the ice planed rocks which skirt the hill completely in all directions. These rocks provide climbs of 'Very Difficult' grade and harder. Some of these begin at the very door of the Coruisk Hut.

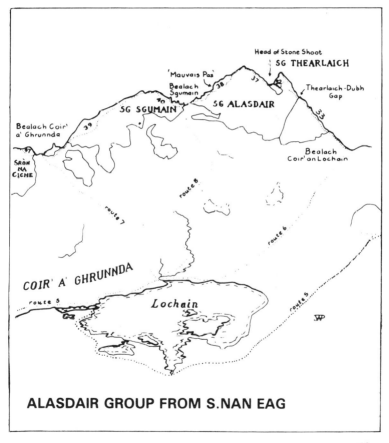

Head of Stone Shoot

SG THEARLAICH

'Mauvais Pas'

Bealach Sgumain

38

37

32

Thearlaich-Dubh Gap

SG SGUMAIN

SG ALASDAIR

40

33

Bealach Coir' a' Ghrunnda

39

SRON NA CICHE

Bealach Coir' an Lochain

route 8

route 7

route 6

COIR' A' GHRUNNDA

route 5

route 5

Lochain

WP

ALASDAIR GROUP FROM S.NAN EAG

SGÙRR ALASDAIR GROUP

SGÙRR THEARLAICH 3,208ft.

Route 32	Via Great Stone Shoot	Glen Brittle	RI
Route 33	South East Ridge	Glen Brittle/Coruisk	RIV
Route 34	North Ridge	Glen Brittle/Coruisk	RII
Route 35	East Face	Coruisk	RII

SGÙRR COIR' AN LOCHAIN 2,491/2,390ft

Route 36	South Ridge		2W/RII

SGÙRR ALASDAIR 3,257ft

Route 37	Via Great Stone Shoot	Glen Brittle	4S
Route 38	South West Ridge	Glen Brittle	RI+ /RIV

SGÙRR SGUMAIN 3,108ft.

Route 39	South Ridge	Glen Brittle	2W
Route 40	East Ridge	Glen Brittle	3S

SRÒN NA CICHE 2,817ft.

Route 41	South West Face	Glen Brittle	2W
Route 42	North East Ridge	Glen Brittle	3S
Route 43	The Cioch 2,336ft.	Glen Brittle	RII

Route 44	**AN SGÙMAN** 806ft	1W
	CEANN NA BEINN 737ft.	2W

These are perhaps the shapeliest peaks in the Cuillin forming a magnificent line along the south wall of the profound Coire Làgan. Before Sheriff Nicolson was immortalised in the name of the highest peak on Skye, the whole range was known as Sgùrr Làgan or Sgùrr Sgumain.

Alasdair and Sgumain are made from hard, brittle, basalt whilst Thearlaich and Sròn na Ciche are mainly gabbro. The Great Stoneshoot lies on a dyke of felsite, and the Thearlaich-Dubh Gap marks another dyke of basalt.

Sg. Alasdair and Sg. Thearlaich from Sg. nan Eag

SGÙRR THEARLAICH 3,208ft.

Known formerly and simply as the North-east Peak of Alasdair until the pioneering exploits of Charles Pilkington were recognised by naming the peak after him, the mountain forms part of the Main Ridge, and a narrow part at that. The east face is a high wall of cliffs but the west, although of rock, is not so high where the neck of scree at the top of the Stone Shoot connects Thearlaich to its higher western neighbour. The simplest way up the mountain Route 32 lies hereabouts and demands rock climbing ability. Mist rules out the peak for all but the expert. The ridges are definitely for climbers also. The south-eastern possesses the infamous Thearlaich-Dubh Gap one of, if not the most difficult of the problems on the Main Ridge Traverse. The west face north of the neck or head of the Great Stone Shoot is seamed with five gullies graded 'Difficult', 'Very Difficult', 'Difficult' 'Very Difficult' and 'Moderate' coming north to south. South of the neck above Coir' a' Ghrunnda, very steep, good rock abounds, a worthy playground for the more competent rock climber, The east face has no recorded routes and a way can be made beneath them to and from the Bealachs north and south of Sgùrr Thearlaich at the expense of dropping 200 feet. On this traverse one encounters a bay of scree. On its left a line may be made slanting left to lead to the south ridge above the Thearlaich-Dubh Gap.

The summit can give extensive views, necessarily restricted on the west by Sgùrr Alasdair. The three Lochains of the South Cuillin are all visible and the south face of Sgùrr Dearg shows well.

Descents. The Stone Shoot approach requires the least climbing and route finding. If making an ascent by this route in mist the place at which the Main Ridge is reached should be noted to facilitate the return. If going for Coruisk it may be wisest for weak climbing parties to return this way and down the Great Stone Shoot to the Bealach Mhic Coinnich, *(Route 9)*, and return over that pass.

32. SGÙRR THEARLAICH from HEAD of GREAT STONE SHOOT RI

Glen Brittle 2¾ miles, 3,250ft of ascent

Follow Route 9 to the Great Stone Shoot. One Cuillin authority reckoned Fheadain a'Cloiches (Chanter of the Stones) would be a fitting name for the treadmill stretching 1,000 feet over one's head. Instead of branching left for the Bealach soldier onwards all the way to the top, walled in by Alasdair (right) and Thearlaich's gullies on the left. A little way beyond the top of the Stone Shoot - 3,135 feet, the angle of the rock wall on the left relents and an easy rock climb of 100 feet or more takes one onto the crest of the Main Ridge a little south of the summit.

33. SGÙRR THEARLAICH - SOUTH EAST RIDGE RIV
(The Thearlaich-Dubh Gap)
Glen Brittle 4¼ miles, 3,350ft of ascent
Coruisk 3¼ miles 3,300ft of ascent

This route is graded by rock climbers as 'Very Difficult'. From either Glen Brittle or Coruisk use Route 6 to Bealach Coir' an Lochain, 2,806ft. Turn north and scramble along the ridge to the pinnacle overhanging the famous Thearlaich-Dubh Gap. A scree covered slab and a steep nose are features of this preliminary section. An abseil of 30 feet takes one into the Gap. To the left, the 'Moderate' and loose Thearlaich-Dubh Gully falls to Coir' a Ghrunnda. To the right a 'Difficult' chimney drops to Coir' an Lochain. Unless we fail to retrieve the rope, our way is up the other side of the gap - an eighty foot wall. The ascent takes a highly polished basalt chimney - almost impossible in the wet. The first 15 feet uses a difficult crack. A small ledge lies above, then the final climb goes up the rest of the corner. Beyond, easy climbing along the ridge brings one to the summit to complete a most difficult rock climb.

34. SGÙRR THEARLAICH - NORTH RIDGE RII
Glen Brittle 2¾ miles, 3,250ft of ascent
Coruisk 3 miles 1 furlong, 3,200ft of ascent

Route 9 will bring parties from either Glen Brittle or Coruisk to Bealach Mhic Coinnich. The succeeding 400 feet demands rock climbing ability to 'Moderate' standard. Turn the first rocks on left (east) then go up a steep wall facing east to an easy section of the ridge. After 60 yards another step has to be taken again on the left. This leads to a steep slab with incut holds which again leads to the crest of an airy ridge which continues narrowly to the summit 300 feet above and 250 yards south of the Bealach.

35. SGÙRR THEARLAICH from
COIR' AN LOCHAIN RII
Coruisk 3 miles 3,200ft of ascent

This 'Easy' rock climbing route was discovered by Harold Raeburn in 1913. A short descent from Bealach Mhic Coinnich on the Coir' an Lochain side over scree leads to the foot of a ridge. The north side is easily climbed before making a direct line for the summit. the fastest approach from Coruisk.

SGÙRR COIR' AN LOCHAIN   2,491 and 2,390ft.

This was the last of Britain's mountain peaks to be climbed. In 1896 Collie, Howell, Naismith and MacKenzie reached the top over the most difficult side! The shepherd at Glen Brittle knew the peak as Sgùrr Dubh a' Choire Lochain but the modern form suggested by Collie and Colin B. Philip has been adopted.

The peak is connected to the Main Ridge at Bealach Mhic Coinnich by an indistinct ridge which narrows at the twin summits from which steep gabbro slabs fall to west, north and east.

36. SGÙRR COIR' AN LOCHAN - SOUTH RIDGE
   2,600ft   2W/RII
   Glen Brittle 3¼ miles 3,150ft of ascent
   Coruisk via Coireachan Ruadha 3 miles 7 furlongs

The South Ridge is reached easily from Bealach Mhic Coinnich *(Route 9)*, 2 miles 5 furlongs from Glen Brittle. A biscuit coloured honeycombed outcrop of peridotite marks the start of the ridge. A low crag across the ridge is easily surmounted by a short chimney at the centre.

Route 6 can also be used by Coruisk based parties. Detour from the route once the slabs barring direct access above the lochain have been turned. From Coruisk Route 10 to Bealach Coire na Banachdich provides a more straightforward approach. Leave the path after entering the left or south branch of Coirèachan Ruadha and turn up under the cliffs of Sgùrr Coir' an Lochain keeping them on the left until the wide South Ridge is reached. On this easy ridge (turn any difficulties on the right) the south 2,491 feet summit is soon underfoot. In mist route finding may be complicated.

Unfortunately the lower summit is held to be the true summit. No doubt shepherds must have visited this point before climbers were active. North of the top, the ridge narrows and the route goes down exposed grassy slabs to an awkward six foot step which lands one in the gap at 2,336 feet. Steep but easy rocks beyond lead directly in 80 feet to a mossy, ancient summit cairn, the most complete vantage point for the mountain sides overlooking Coir' Uisg.

The gully falling west of the gap is a 'Difficult' rock climb and its partner falling to Coir' an Lochain is not graded in rock climbing guide books, but looks almost as steep.

SGÙRR ALASDAIR   3,257ft.

Until 1965 official maps credited the mountain with an altitude of 3,309 feet. Indeed some small scale maps and atlases still carry the figure. Since 1923 the S.M.C. accepted Doctor Barlow's more accurate figure of 3,254 feet. The peak is still an awe inspiring one, especially when seen across Coire Làgan. The face which overlooks Loch Làgan boasts two classic rock climbing routes of 'Hard Difficult' standard of great antiquity and the results of brave pioneering by Professor Collie and the Abraham fraternity.

The summit is small and very airy. The best part of an obviously extensive view is difficult to decide upon. Just enjoy it all if conditions permit. To the north Sgùrr Dearg's loose but often sunlit flanks topped by the improbable Inaccessible Pinnacle compels one's attention.

Descents. The South-east Ridge is the easiest but even here care is essential. Mist should in any case rule out any ascent. On reaching the Stone Shoot check your direction. Note the upper section has been eroded and the steep bedrock has been exposed. The gully going down the wrong side (south) plunges over a high precipice above Coire' a' Ghrunndda.

37.   SGÙRR ALASDAIR – EAST RIDGE from GREAT STONE SHOOT   4S
Glen Brittle 2¾ miles   3,300ft of ascent

This ascent of the reigning peak must be one of the most popular in the Cuillin, being the easiest way of attaining the highest summit on Skye. Take the path from Glen Brittle described in Route 9 then ascend the Great Stone Shoot. Firmer footing will be found on the edges beneath the perpendicular enclosing walls. On the descent the small stones in the centre will speed the competent scree runner. The scree extends for fully 1,300 feet and is very exasperating. Eventually one arrives at the head of the gully and emerges into daylight with a view of Coir' a' Ghrunnda (3135 feet). Turn right here and ascend a

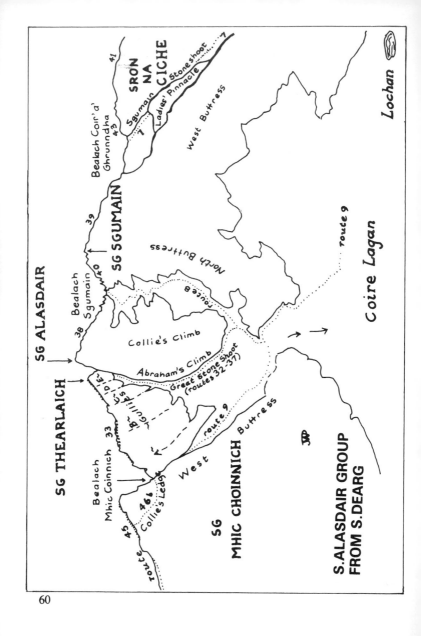

SRON NA CICHE

41

Sguman

Bealach Coir' a' Ghrunndha
43

7 Stoneshoot

7

Ladies' Pinnacle

West Buttress

SG SGUMAIN

39

SG ALASDAIR

Bealach Sgumain
40

38

North Buttress

route 8

route 8

Collie's Climb

Abraham's Climb

Great Stone Shoot (routes 32-37)

SG THEARLAICH

route 9

route 9

route 9

route A

route B

route C

Bealach Mhic Coinnich
33

West Buttress

45

46

Collie's Ledge

SG MHIC CHOINNICH

route 9

Coire Lagan

Lochan

S. ALASDAIR GROUP FROM S. DEARG

long narrow ridge of basalt to the smallest summit in the Cuillin. The last section comprises a difficult and exposed 130 feet scramble.

38. SGÙRR ALASDAIR SOUTH WEST RIDGE
RI/RIV
Glen Brittle 2 miles 5 furlongs   3,300ft of ascent

Route 8 will conduct the climber to the high Bealach Sgumain 3,023 feet. The ridge (left) to the highest peak begins with some crumbling pinnacles which are avoided on the south. A slight loss of altitude being incurred. An open corner is taken and one goes left to the crest. The famous Mauvais Pas is on the left for those taking the direct route at 'Hard Very Difficult' grade. Modern rock climbing guides make no reference to the easy option that lies to the right and turns the twenty foot wall crossing the face before one by a chimney. The last 200 feet are loose and steep but not too difficult up the exposed flank.

SGÙRR SGUMAIN   3,108ft.

Sgùrr Alasdair overshadows its neighbour which still is worthy of a visit. The North Buttress provides a long basaltic climb but the West Buttress is harder in both senses of the word. The east flank is broken. Minor pinnacles grace the broad summit.

The prospect into Coire Làgan is awesome.

The best descent is the more gradual way down the South Ridge and the Sgumain Stone Shoot to the base of Sròn na Ciche whence the well trodden path conducts one to Glen Brittle.(*Route 7.*)

39. SGÙRR SGUMAIN - SOUTH RIDGE   2W
Glen Brittle 2½ miles 3,150ft of ascent

From Glen Brittle take Route 7 up the Sgumain Stone Shoot to Bealach Coir' a' Ghrunnda 2,759 feet 2 miles 3 furlongs. Turn left up the easy open ridge with a mere 350 feet of ascent. No more than uphill walking is encountered.

40. SGÙRR SGUMAIN - EAST RIDGE   3S
Glen Brittle 2 miles 5 furlongs 3,150ft of ascent

The steep tiring screes leading to Bealach Sgumain are described under Route 8. From the col - 3,023 feet, a very short scramble leads beyond a subsidiary summit to the highest top overlooking Coire

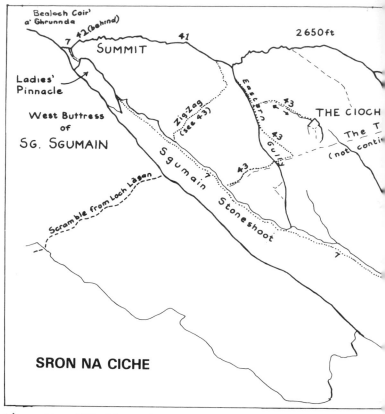

Làgan. Turn difficulties on the south side.

SRÒN NA CICHE 2,817ft.

The lowly eminence forming the last top of the important lateral ridge extending south-west from the Main Ridge gives simple walking over its broad crest from the Glen Brittle to Coruisk path via the shore. However, its flank overlooking Coire Làgan is composed of the largest compact cliff in the Cuillin. A mile wide and over a thousand feet high, it boasts a plethora of routes of all difficulties which are popular thanks to their accessibility from Glen Brittle.

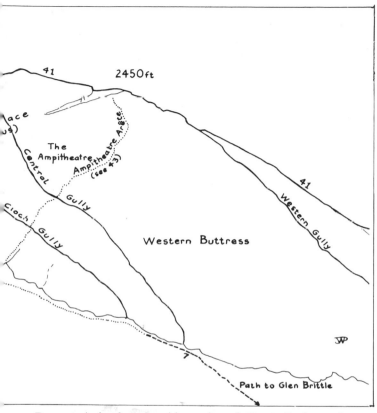

Descent. A simple and rapid way down is Route 41, the south-west flank.

41 SRÒN NA CICHE - SOUTH WEST FLANK 2W
Glen Brittle 3 miles 2,900ft of ascent

There can be no simpler ascent in the Cuillin. Follow Route 4 from the camp-site until Allt Coire Làgan is crossed at 1 mile 7 furlongs, then head up the stone and grass ridge avoiding crags on the left. You are now on a broad tilted plateau which gradually narrows as height is gained. The 2,000 feet ascent is enlivened by the sensational

63

views taken down the precipice and detours to avoid gullies cutting into the ridge.

42. SRÒN NA CICHE from THE SGUMAIN STONE SHOOT 3S
Glen Brittle 2 miles 3 furlongs 2,800ft of ascent

Bealach Coir' a' Ghrunnda is reached (*Route 7*) and your summit lies not a hundred yards away to the south-west, so turn right. Some low rock walls are avoidable to the left, otherwise no difficulties occur.

43. SRÒN NA CICHE VIA THE CIOCH RII
Glen Brittle 2½ miles 2,800ft of ascent

A' Chioch was christened by John MacKenzie after he had accompanied Collie on its first ascent. It is included in this itinerary up this face of the mountain for completeness. The whole enterprise should be regarded as a very long and 'Difficult' rock climb requiring a rope plus an experienced leader, though it may be said to constitute one of the easier ways up the cliff.

From Glen Brittle Route 7 is taken to the base of the cliff below the Cioch, a jutting prow half way up the 1,000 feet face. Continue to the left passing the breaks in the cliff formed by the Little Gully and the Eastern Gully. This last gully has a 'Severe' rock pitch which we now have to circumvent. Continue up the stone shoot until a break in the steep cliff leads onto The Terrace which is followed to the right across the continuation of Eastern Gully to the base of the obvious and massive clean Cioch Slab. Climb some deep cracks leftward across this and enter Eastern Gully's easier continuation. Climb the gully for 50 feet. Now traverse to the right towards the Cioch itself along a shelf leading slightly downhill across the top of the Slab to a narrow neck of rock connecting the main face to the Cioch itself. A chimney on the left of the Cioch or holds right of it conducts one to the flat summit. A memorable view point at 2,336 feet.

To attain the top of the mountain return to the Eastern Gully. A deep cave formed by a huge boulder is encountered. Scramble into the gloom, the left wall then a long step and a good heave gets one above the obstacle. The boulder filled gully divides higher up. The right branch gives least resistance. Before the top a last problem is overcome by going below some more wedged rocks. The summit lies 150 yards to the left.

Over sixty routes exist on this vast cliff and among the easiest are Zig Zag on Eastern Buttress ('Moderate') which crosses its east side from the stone shoot to the crest. Amphitheatre Arête, also 'Moderate', starts at the lowest rocks of Cioch Buttress and goes up ledges crossing both Cioch Gully and Central Gully. From the Amphitheatre the arête is reached on the right by going across slabs. Western Gully has one 'Moderate' pitch and many easy ones amidst a lot of scree.

44. AN SGÙMAN 806ft. 1W
    CEANN NA BEINN 737ft. 2W

These rounded humps belong topographically, if not geologically to the Sròn na Ciche Ridge. An Sgùman is made from peridotite (west half) and basalt and lies a quarter-mile south of the shore path *Route 4*. 2½ miles out from Glen Brittle.

Ceann na Beinn lies central to the remote boglands over-lying dolerite and basalt. It might be visited in conjunction with a tour of inspection of the sea cliffs on the shore of Loch Brittle, though it lies a tiring mile and a half from both An Sgùman and the sea.

SGÙRR MHIC COINNICH   3,111ft.

Route 45 NW Ridge from Bealach Làgan Glen Brittle 4S

Route 46 S.Face, Collie's Ledge, King's Chimney,
             Glen Brittle/Coruisk RII or IV

When Charles Pilkington's party made the first ascent in 1884 from Bealach Làgan they jokingly referred to the mountain as 'Pic MacKenzie' after their famous guide, the name has stuck, though in its Gaelic form. Steep rock defends the summit on all sides. A gently sloping narrow ridge suddenly plunges to a col to the south. The broken western basaltic face above Coire Làgan boasts a 1,000 foot rock climb, Western Buttress. Girdling the summit on this face is a narrow platform or ledge discovered by Collie in 1890. The other, eastern face is not quite as high but is equally difficult, more so at the northern end where some of the Cuillin's most impressive rocks and climbs are to be found. Furthermore no easy way exists to the dips between Mhic Coinnich and Sgùrr Dearg from the Coruisk side. Rotten Gully is not even recommended to rock climbers. A grass rake starting below the summit can be followed to the right to a nick in the ridge's outline, but this may be very exposed. The cliffs on this east face and Sgùrr Coir' an Lochain are gabbro while a belt of peridotite runs between. Altogether a peak reserved for rock climbers only.

Descents. The North-West Ridge to Bealach Làgan is much easier than the drop to Bealach Mhic Coinnich which will require an abseil. Bealach Làgan gives access only to Glen Brittle unless a party is prepared to continue over Sgùrr Dearg to Bealach Coire na Banachdich *(Route 10)* or traverse back across the western base of the mountain over steep loose terrain to Bealach Mhic Coinnich *(Route 9).*

45. NORTH WEST RIDGE, SGÙRR MHIC COINNICH 4S

Glen Brittle 2 miles 7 furlongs   3,300ft of ascent

This standard ascent above Loch Làgan 1,860 feet is reached from the valley via Route 9 (2 miles 3 furlongs). A path north of the Lochan is taken to the An Stac screes which are ascended to a col, Bealach Làgan, 2,690 feet, which lies a short distance left or north west of the *lowest* point between An Stac and our peak. These screes are not used a great deal and can still give an enjoyable means of fast descent to those expert or silly enough to indulge in scree running. Once on the Main Ridge we go right and over a minor hump then begin the long, narrow ridge of rock without any significant difficulty but containing a great deal of scrambling. The top is obvious, the drop beyond is very significant!

46. SGÙRR MHIC COINNICH from BEALACH MHIC COINNICH RII or IV

Glen Brittle 2¾ miles   3,200ft of ascent
Coruisk hut 4 miles   3,200ft of ascent

From Bealach the 'south face' of the mountain constitutes one of the major obstacles on the Main Ridge, Collie's Ledge overcomes the problem, though indirectly. This 'Easy' but exposed rock climb starts 20 feet above the bealach following a ledge slanting up and left across the 1,000 feet face overlooking Coire Làgan. This continues until it reaches the ridge some way north of the summit. Another grassier traversing line exists below Collie's Ledge reached by descending a little way from the bealach. These 'Moderate' rock climbs were superseded in 1898 by the efforts of W.Wickham King in climbing his eponymous chimney, a 'Difficult' but direct way to the top.

top.

Start this route 60 feet directly above the Bealach. The chimney or corner is left beneath an overhang which is avoided by a steep, smooth slab on the right. A little scrambling remains before the top is reached.

SGÙRR DEARG

SGÙRR DEARG 3,209ft.
(**Sròn Dearg** 2,090ft **and Sgùrr Dearg Beag** 3,040ft)

Route 47	W.Ridge via Sròn Dearg and Sgùrr Dearg Beag	Glen Brittle	3S
Route 48	N. Ridge	Glen Brittle/Coruisk	1W
Route 49	S. Face (An Stac)	Glen Brittle	2W

INACCESSIBLE PINNACLE 3,234ft.

Route 50	E. Ridge	RII
Route 51	West Ridge	RIII

Sgùrr Dearg is one of the more important of the Cuillin summits. It is overtopped only by the monarch, Sgùrr Alasdair and is the highest point on the Main Ridge and like its rival is composed mainly of basalt. Although a popular peak and worthy of an ascent by the fell walker he may return disappointed because the Inaccessible Pinnacle overtops the 'summit' by 25 feet. This remarkable monolith consists of a narrow wall of rock not a hundred yards long, perched on the sloping eastern roof of the 'summit' ridge which runs north - south. The west end of this Inaccessible Pinnacle, that is the end dropping just short of, and nearest the 'summit' cairn, is perpendicular and 80 feet high. The further end falls in a steep narrow ridge to a lesser drop.

The mountain which supports this exciting feature has three faces and three ridges. The ridges generally provide the ways to the top for the walker while rock climbers can revel in good long routes on the three contrasting rock faces. The north west face provides the principal feature in the view from Glen Brittle Hut windows. In mist or strong evening light the existence of the Window Tower is made apparent. In these conditions one can discern the remarkable holes

Sg.Mhic Choinnich from Sg.Alasdair. Collie's Ledge can be seen rising across the summit rocks.

piercing the summit of a pointed rock tower perched half way up the steep face of the mountain which boasts several interesting climbs of medium grade for climbers with half-a-day to spare. The Tower can be visited via an easy rock gully reaching behind its neck. The north east face of Sgùrr Dearg is strictly for the birds or extremely good cragsmen - a dark forbidding, overhanging 1,000 feet unbroken line of cliffs. The open, sunny but loose south face carries ribbons of rock falling to Coire Làgan amidst large areas of steep scree. The ridges are dealt with on the route descriptions below.

Descents. Best and quickest for Glen Brittle is the West Ridge. Take a curving course to the right on the southern crest of the 'summit' ridge to the narrowing ridge of the Dearg Beag. Cairns are helpful beyond and one need not stray over to the ridge on the right which ends above the Window Buttress. An hour should suffice for the journey by a hungry party.

Those bound for Coruisk have Hobson's Choice, the walk down to Bealach Coir' a' Banachdich Route 10 which curves north west then north around the head of the terrific crags overhanging the loose screes on the east side of the mountain.

47. SGÙRR DEARG VIA WEST RIDGE
over Sròn Dearg and Sgùrr Dearg Beag 3S
Glen Brittle 2¼ miles   3,300ft of ascent

From the bridge between the BMC Hut and Glen Brittle House, paths running on either side of the burn which drains Coire na Banachdich converge by the water pipes 200 yards upstream. The well trodden path rises over the moor to the right of the burn. Use a branch staying left so you gain a peep at Eas Mòr, then turn right once more for 200 yards on. Hence a path turns left from that leading to Coire Làgan and mounts the broad ridge directly ahead. Scree comes underfoot as you head for the first objective - an eminence along the ridge where the northern flanks begin to assert themselves and merge into the cliffs of Window Buttress. This is Sròn Dearg 2,090 feet and 1 mile 5 furlongs out from the road. The well trodden way continues toward another minor summit, Sgùrr Dearg Beag 3,040 feet and 2 miles from Glen Brittle, the ridge hereabouts narrows considerably and some easy scrambling ensues along some exhilarating up and down work on the crest of all things. This work continues towards the parent summit circling to the left while the scrambling gets easier. The largish cairn is perched on an apex which pitches steeply to the

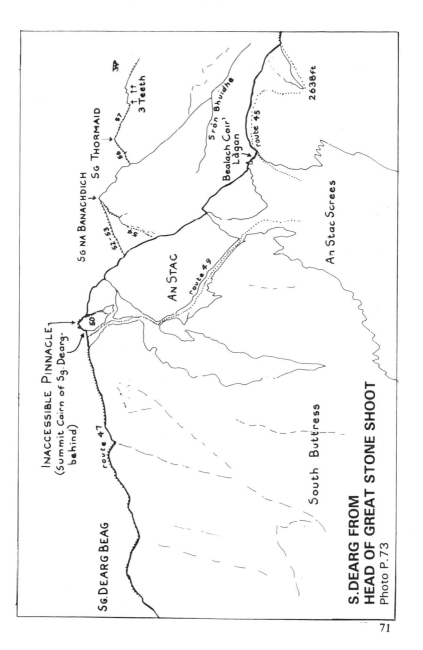

S. DEARG FROM
HEAD OF GREAT STONE SHOOT
Photo P.73

SP

3 Teeth

57

56

Sg THORMAID

Sgùrr na Banachdich

Sròn Bhuidhe

Bealach Coir'
Lagan

route 45

2638ft

52-53

54-5

An Stac

route 49

An Stac Screes

Inaccessible Pinnacle
(Summit Cairn of Sg. Dearg-
behind)

50

route 47

Sg. Dearg Beag

South Buttress

71

right. The view as might be expected is extensive but the Coire Làgan Faces of the other giants hold the most attention. Sgùrr na Banachdich is seen end on but Sgùrr a' Ghreadaidh's massiveness is apparent beyond.

48. SGÙRR DEARG - NORTH RIDGE
from Bealach Coire na Banachdich   1W

Glen Brittle 2 miles 3 furlongs,
Coruisk 4 miles 1 furlong   3,300ft of ascent

Route 10 conducts the fell walker from Glen Brittle (scramble) or Coruisk to the Bealach 2,791 feet. 2¼ and 4 miles from the respective starting points. By and large the way is an easy walk to the summit, avoiding the massive drops on the left where necessary.

49. SGÙRR DEARG VIA THE AN STAC SCREES (SOUTH EAST RIDGE)   2W

Glen Brittle 2 miles 7 furlongs   3,300ft of ascent

No practicable route for walkers based at Coruisk joins this way up Sgùrr Dearg which generally follows the south east ridge on its Coire Làgan side, avoiding the steep rocks supporting the minor summit of An Stac 3,130 feet. This name was probably the original title of Sgùrr Dearg's Pinnacle as John MacKenzie referred to An Stac as Sgùrr na Calleag.

From Loch Làgan the path up the corrie continues on the north side of the burn towards Bealach Làgan before petering out amongst the loose rock and scree up which you now climb. An opening between the crags appears, going up to the left about 200 feet below the crest of the Main Ridge. Yet more scree is followed below the south west wall of An Stac's imposing rocks. This line is continued for a climb of 700 feet until one meets the south wall of the Inaccessible Pinnacle. From here you may turn right and cross easy rock and bag An Stac. Otherwise, traverse up and left below the Inaccessible Pinnacle to the summit just on the west along a ledge.

Main Ridge parties arriving at Bealach Làgan from Sgùrr Mhic Coinnich should turn the first obstacle on the left and continue the route over the screes described, though An Stac's steep face can be climbed direct on 'Difficult' rock. This part of the ridge was descended in 1892.

Sgurr Dearg and the Inaccessible Pinnacle from the top of the Great Stone Shoot (see diagram p.71)

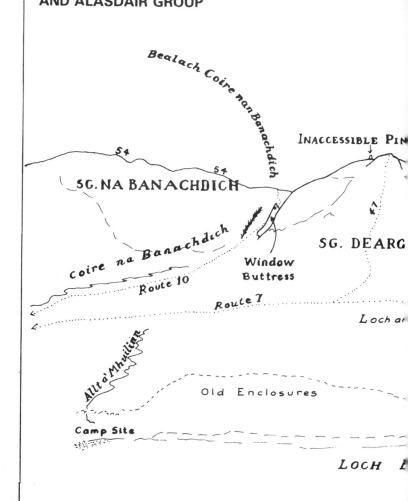

WESTERN ASPECT OF S.DEARG
AND ALASDAIR GROUP

Bealach Coire nan Banachdich

INACCESSIBLE PIN

54

54

SG. NA BANACHDICH

SG. DEARG

Coire na Banachdich

Window Buttress

Route 10

Route 7

Loch an

Allt a'Mhuilinn

Old Enclosures

Camp Site

LOCH

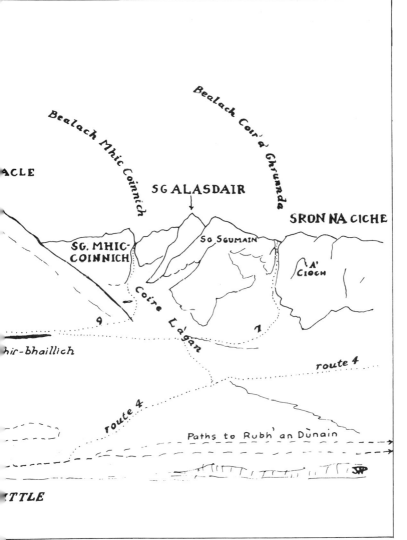

THE INACCESSIBLE PINNACLE 3,234ft.

The name and an altitude of 3,212 feet was accorded the feature by the Admiralty in the 1850's. Locally it was known as the Old Man of Skye or An Stac.

50. EAST RIDGE RII

The seafarers' claim of inviolability was broken some 30 years later by Charles and Lawrence Pilkington with John MacKenzie who climbed it by this route. The loose rocks that predominated have long since been cleared and now the way is highly polished if obvious. Unless you are an experienced climber armed with rope and slings and unconcerned with 3,000 feet of exposure consider the rock out of bounds. The huge slab on which the Pinnacle stands slopes over into the boundless depths of Coireachan Ruadha. On the sheerer south side of the rock there is less exposure where the route from Coire Làgan to the summit passes by.

The East Ridge is reached up the south wall several yards from the bottom end where an easy groove line gives access to the crest. 'Moderate' climbing with one nasty steep move is encountered during the 200 feet ascent. The exposure on either hand is sensational. The summit consists of a massive 8 foot high boulder perched on end and precariously balanced on some lesser debris. This was known as the Bolster Stone.

51. WEST 'RIDGE' RIII

This is the 80 foot drop onto the slabs sloping east of the 'summit' cairn. The holds are very polished. The climbing guides grade it 'Difficult'. The crux is an awkward move between sloping shelves halfway up.

Descents. Either of the routes must be reversed or more usually an abseil is made down the shorter west end. A (new) sling threaded in the stones supporting the Bolster Stone serves as an anchor for this rope manoeuvre.

SGÙRR NA BANACHDICH GROUP

AN DIALLAID 2,340ft and SGÙRR NA BANACHDICH
Route 52 North West Ridge via An Diallaid Glen Brittle 2W

SGÙRR NAN GOBHAR 2,069ft - SGÙRR NA BANACHDICH
Route 53 West Ridge via Sgùrr nan Gobhar Glen Brittle 3S

SGÙRR NA BANACHDICH 3,166ft.

Route 54 South Ridge from Bealach na Banachdich
Glen Brittle/Coruisk 4S
Route 55 North Ridge Glen Brittle/Coruisk 3S

SGÙRR THORMAID 3.040ft.
Route 56 South West Ridge Coruisk 4S
Route 57 North East Ridge Glen Brittle 3S

From the most westerly turn in the Main Ridge, an important lateral spur runs west to dominate Glen Brittle. At the junction of these ridges lies Sgùrr na Banachdich, one of the easiest Munroes in the Cuillin. Some authorities claimed the correct name was 'Bannachaig' meaning 'peak of the milkmaid'. A pity 'peak of the smallpox' now holds general currency. Because the gabbro hereabouts is badly pitted the name has stuck. Even if the maid may not have taken her stool and pail to the corrie above Eas Mór perhaps the valley may have been a favourite excursion during hours spared from minding the cows. The group in question is composed mainly of gabbro. The only peridotite forms the base of Srón Bhuidhe. The summit of Srón Bhuidhe is basalt as are the uppermost rocks of Sgùrr Thormaid and An Diallaid. The ridge of Sgùrr nan Gobhar is alternately gabbro and basalt.

AN DIALLAID 2,340ft

The three summits of this outlier of Banachdich are not much more than successive platforms overlooking a steep northern face of rock harbouring several gully climbs.

SGÙRR NA BANACHDICH 3,166ft.

The simple ascents from the west are so tame that the surprise view from the very summit down the 600 feet overlooking the Coruisk face is traumatic. Admiration overcomes horror as one gazes over the streams and water of Coir' Uisg to a panorama which includes both the Red and the Black Cuillin. Here is possibly the best vantage point of Coire a' Ghreadaidh but this basin is open and boasts few outstanding features.

The east face consists of steep terraced cliffs debarring access from Coruisk. The Main Ridge boasts several tops. Those to the south have preserved some anonymity but the old north east top now serves to honour the Cuillin's greatest pioneer; Professor Collie and is known in Gaelic as the Peak of Norman. The west face forms an unrelenting head wall of crag and scree above Coire na Banachdich. The west ridge culminates in Sgùrr nan Gobhar. Steep scree and grass lie between the peaks on the Coire na Banachdich side of this west ridge but the north wall is generally unbroken except where a rather vague subsidiary spur juts into Coir' a' Ghreadaidh to the Saddle - An Diallaid. This top encloses a minor hollow which gives access to the Main Ridge.

Descents. For Coruisk in mist descend the way you came up, as both alternatives are complicated. For Glen Brittle the west ridge is quickest and safest though care is required in hitting off the correct place to depart from the ridge to proceed into Coir' an Eich or Coire na Banachdich. The Coir' an Eich is found by encircling to the right (north) until one meets the ups and downs of An Diallaid. Go left and downhill then simply follow the burn down to the path in Coire a' Ghreadaidh.

52. BANACHDICH - WEST RIDGE
VIA AN DIALLAID 2W
Glen Brittle 2½ miles 3,200ft of ascent

'Professor Forbes expressed the belief that Banachdich might perhaps be accessible on the Brittle side'. He was right. This is an all - walking route. Gloveless summiteers need not get cold hands on cold days if their trousers have pockets.

At Glen Brittle Youth Hostel a path leaves the road to run above the rocky right (south) bank of the Coire a Ghreadaidh Burn. This well trodden track ends in a flattish hollow where the stream draining

*Sg.na Banachdich and Sg.a'Ghreadaidh
from the top of the Great Stone Shoot*

Coir' an Eich joins the main burn. This tributary is followed again on the right (true left) bank. Here the way is quite steep as one picks a way over vegetatious slopes. When the gradient eases again half the vertical distance to Banachdich has been climbed. From another hollow (Coir' an Eich) a ridge to the left of the stream has developed. On this ridge small scree and grass affords a less arduous surface to negotiate and you obtain a bird's-eye view of Coire a' Ghreadaidh as a bonus. Thus An Diallaid's three tops are reached 2 miles out from the hostel.

Striking south and uphill we skirt the crags surrounding the Coire a' Ghreadaidh until we join the broad loose ridge leading steadily up to the parent peak from Sgùrr Gobhar. The summit cairn lies over on the right when the summit ridge is gained.

53. BANACHDICH – WEST RIDGE VIA SGÙRR NAN GOBHAR 3S
Glen Brittle 2¼ miles   3,250ft of ascent

Sgùrr nan Gobhar is a shapely cone of scree or rock thrust up high above Glen Brittle, its slopes sweep unbroken to the road. The terminating point is guarded by a circle of crags some 500 feet high. To the south west in a line with the 'House' and Hut at Glen Brittle these crags have been inundated by a field of screes and this provides a rapid means of descent for avid scree runners. The base of the scree lies at 1,000 feet. A rough track of sorts leads through rough pasture across the lower slopes from the Memorial Hut, but you can pick a way over the heathery slopes from any point on the road to the screes. One or two cliffs break the continuity of a direct ascent but they are easily avoided. However, cliffs do bar access from north and south but apart from Goat's Gully a 'Difficult' climb, no climbing routes exist on either face. Beyond the summit of Gobhar (1¾ miles and 2,100 feet) the ridge is broken by shallow gaps where dykes of basalt have weathered. The scrambling entailed is straightforward. Beyond the first serious piece of scrambling a quarter mile after Gobhar, a scree rake slants down towards the Banachdich Corrie and provides a way down if one requires a return to Glen Brittle without retracing one's steps. Continue up steadily over at least two rocky outcrops with a steep rock on the left and scree on the right until the ridge broadens out to a wide stony plateau beyond the junction with that leading to An Diallaid where Route 52 is joined and followed to the summit.

54. SOUTH RIDGE, SGÙRR NA BANACHDICH 4S

Glen Brittle 2½ miles 3,250ft of ascent
Coruisk 4¼ miles 3,250ft of ascent

Bealach Coire na Banachdich is easily reached via Route 10 from Glen Brittle (2¼ miles or Coruisk 4 miles). The half-mile ridge involves some exposed scrambling much of it serious, unless several minor tops are avoided on the west (left) by still fairly exposed open slopes. Once embarked on the ridge the walker must not attempt to descend until the summit is reached. Immediately north of the Bealach is the summit of Sròn Bhuidhe, the yellow nose. The upper rocks harbour some rock climbs and are known as The Twins. The next summit the 'third top' attains the magic 3,000 feet level. The 3,089 feet 'second top' provides the most difficult part of the ridge. Nearly a hundred feet of descent beyond leads to the last gap. A little scrambling remains but the cliffs on the right have gained in height and pitch on the approach to the summit plateau upon which the cairn is poised over the abyss.

55. SGÙRR NA BANACHDICH NORTH RIDGE 3S

Coruisk 4¼ miles 3,200ft of ascent
Glen Brittle 2¾ miles 3,200ft of ascent

'Bealach Thormaid' is the gap at 2,914 feet between Sgùrr Banachdich and Thormaid. The Coruisk approach is the easiest.

From the hut at Scavaig follow Route 10 as far as the confluence of streams draining the two main Coireachan Ruadha branches (3 miles 400 feet). The one to the left (south) is used by the tracks leading up to Bealach Coire na Banachdich. We follow that flowing from the hollow between Sgùrrs Banachdich and Thormaid. A direct ascent can be made to the gap between these peaks. The way alongside the stream is straightforward and gradually steepens as a break in a line of rocks is crossed. Loose screes lie between rock walls on the last pull to Bealach Thormaid. (4 miles).

From Glen Brittle ascend Route 11 towards An Dorus until the lower slopes of Sgùrr Eadar da Choire are reached. Bear right and enter the right-hand upper branch of the main corrie having avoided huge ice-planed slabs washed by several watercourses. Onto the

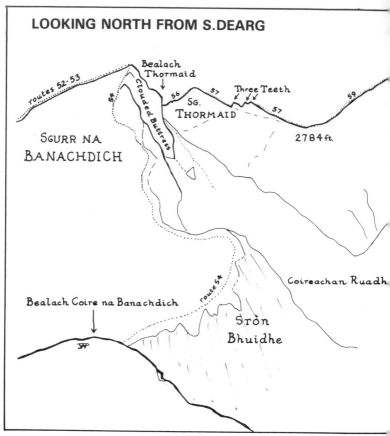

LOOKING NORTH FROM S.DEARG

routes 52-53

Bealach Thormaid

Three Teeth

56   57   57   59

SG. THORMAID

SGURR NA BANACHDICH

Clouded Buttress

2784 ft.

Coireachan Ruadh

route 54

Bealach Coire na Banachdich

Sròn Bhuidhe

broad stony shelf you have gained debouch three large gullies seaming the west face of Sgùrr a' Ghreadaidh. 50 yards right of the right-hand one (Diagonal Gully), progress may be made up a rake slanting up to the right, which passes just beneath an immense overhang of rock below the summit rocks of Thormaid. Easy climbing is encountered at the beginning of the route and at the end of the rake where one turns left into the mountain up a shallow gully. The gully brings one to the gap. The lower section of the gully is steeper and

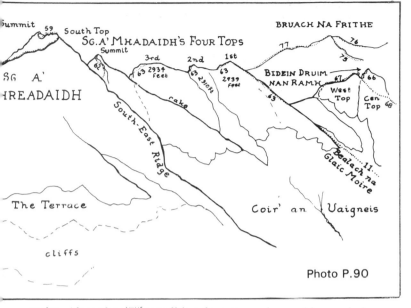

Photo P.90

rocky. Altogether an expedition for seasoned scramblers and clear days.

The 400 yards of steepish scree begins with a couple of pinnacles in the gap both being turned on the west. The larger can be taken direct by scramblers. The summit has a gable end to the north so stay on the right or west up scree up to and along the upper section of the ridge.

SGÙRR THORMAID   3,040ft.

This peak is difficult of access and requires rock climbing ability to traverse the Main Ridge with confidence. A fine little mountain though overshadowed by its neighbours.

Descents. The south ridge and a re-ascent of Sgùrr na Banachdich's North Ridge is the safest way off the peak if bound for Glen Brittle. The south ridge and a descent of the Coireachan Ruadha screes makes the simplest way off for parties based at Coruisk.

56. SOUTH-WEST RIDGE THORMAID   4S

Glen Brittle 2 miles 3 furlongs 3,100ft of ascent
Coruisk 4 miles 3,100ft of ascent

From Coruisk or Glen Brittle the approaches described in Route 55
conduct you to Bealach Thormaid between Sgùrrs Thormaid and
Banachdich. After passing some broken rocks along the ridge, climb
on well scratched good holds just over on the Glen Brittle side. This
takes you onto the exposed roof of the mountain. Sloping ledges
provide a grassy seat for the impressive views.

57. SGÙRR THORMAID
NORTH-EAST RIDGE   3S RII

Glen Brittle 2 miles 3 furlongs   3,100ft of ascent

Another slightly more difficult means of climbing Thormaid from
Glen Brittle direct involves following Route 55 onto the rake right of
Diagonal Gully. After a short distance one gains ground leading left
to the Thormaid - Ghreadaidh gap by a short but 'Moderate' rock
climb leading up and left over an awkward rib. Other ways may be
possible to climbers hereabouts. Steep rocks fall from this col (2,784ft
2¼ miles) on the Coruisk side.

The scramble along the Main Ridge to the summit is most
interesting but rather exposed, especially at the top. The Three
Teeth, three small pinnacles which can provide 'Very Difficult'
scrambling can be turned on the west side by an easy slaggy ledge
formed by a dolerite sill. The 30ft high fangs offer no problem to
a rock climber. The first two form a pair with hardly a gap between.
The last one, nearest the summit, has a steep drop immediately
beyond its top. The line of the sill is continued beyond towards the
summit's exposed ridge, grassy slabs are poised above the 400 feet
cliff, constituting the Coruisk face of the peak. A steeper more
broken western side breaks off into a huge, unseen overhang -
perhaps the largest to be found on the western side of the Main
Ridge.

SGÙRR A' GHREADAIDH

SGÙRR A' GHREADAIDH 3,192ft

| Route 58 | North Ridge | Glen Brittle/Coruisk | RI |
| Route 59 | South Ridge | Glen Brittle | 4S |

SGÙRR EADAR DA CHOIRE 2,650ft

| Route 60 | West Face and continuation to Sgùrr a' Ghreadaidh | Glen Brittle | RII |

Wholly composed of gabbro-from Glen Brittle, Sgùrr a' Ghreadaidh has been described as the 'Great Central Dome of the Coolin' by an old mountaineer, Mr. W. Douglas. When viewed from the valleys its simple though massive form is certainly dominating. However, there is nothing dome-like to anyone traversing the knife-edge connecting the twin summits on the highest peak on the Main Ridge north of Sgùrr Dearg. Ghreadaidh remained unclimbed until 1870 when W.Newton Tribe made his ascent.

The 1,000 feet Western Face is steep but loose and harbours three gullies:- Hidden, Vanishing and Diagonal Gullies which (from north to south) are graded 'Very Difficult', 'Difficult' and 'Easy' respectively. Left or north of these, an important ridge juts out into Coire a' Ghreadaidh and supports a separate summit:- Sgùrr Eadar da Choire. Further north again is the basalt gully falling from Eag Dubh, which is a rock climbers way graded 'Easy'. North once more and we have at least one break in the wall of rock encircling Coire a' Ghreadaidh and this is the scree shoot leading the walker to An Dorus - 'The Door', which demarcates the peaks of Mhadaidh and Ghreadaidh *(Route 11)*.

The eastern face of our mountain offers even less hope to the walker. Even the easiest route consists of Britain's longest continuous rock climb - the South East Ridge, climbed by Professor Collie and Mr. Howell in 1896. The Terrace halfway up this face has 'Severe' routes on the slabby rocks below and the steep face above, and cannot be traversed except by roped experts. The Eag Dubh Gully on this Coir' an Uaigneis side is a 'Difficult' route and even An Dorus is a scramble. *(Route 11)*.

The view from the elegant summit is one of the finest in the Cuillin. A breathtaking scene is that of the Coruisk basin lying at full stretch beneath ones toes. Loch Scavaig and Sgùrr na Stri complete a scene without equal in Scotland.

Descents. The simplest way down is the North Ridge and the approaches to An Dorus *Route 11*. Take account of the 'false ridge' or Wart overhanging the east face or you will be poised over a void. Below it, slabs on the east side avoid a steep and narrow section, cross the narrow gap of Eag Dubh and continue to An Dorus proper.

58.   SGÙRR A' GHREADAIDH FROM AN DORUS (NORTH RIDGE)   RI

Glen Brittle 2¾ miles   3,250ft of ascent
Coruisk Hut 4¼ miles   3,250ft of ascent

An Dorus is reached from Glen Brittle Youth Hostel 2 miles 5 furlongs and the Coruisk Hut 4 miles by taking Route 11. From An Dorus a 15 foot rock step is encountered immediately. This is the crux of the ascent and is awkward. A slabby crest of rock leads to the 2,960 feet top beyond which is Eag Dubh, a gap 70 feet lower reaches down on the left (east). The south wall of the Eag is turned on the left also. Beyond some more slabs is the wall of the wart, a huge 'false ridge' below the summit. this is avoided by ledges on the right (west) just before the final easy rise to the northern or highest summit, where the ridge narrows to a knife-edge.

59.   SOUTH-WEST RIDGE, SGÙRR A' GHREADAIDH 4S

Glen Brittle 2½ miles   3,200ft of ascent

Route 57 or a traverse over Sgùrr Thormaid from Sgùrr Banachdich will land you at the commencement of the South-west ridge at the dip at 2,784, 3 furlongs from the summit. The mountain is imposing from here. Bubbly rocks best taken on the left begin this enjoyable and exposed scramble. An easy bouldery section follows, then the ridge becomes rocky again, broad to begin then narrowing to the south top at 3,181 feet. The level summit ridge will be seen curving gradually to the higher, northern one. The traverse of this sensational knife-edge is one of the most enjoyable (or horrifying) scrambles in Britain. The backcloth is delectable but one's pre-occupation should be with safe progress and not the view, unless you are 'resting' on a handy ledge!

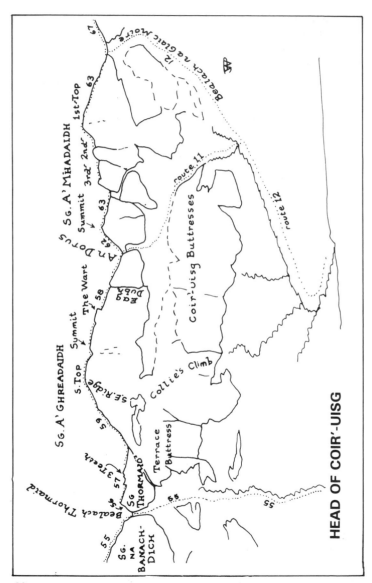

HEAD OF COIR'-UISG

60. SGÙRR EADAR DA CHOIRE RII or 2W/RII
AND CONTINUATION TO SGÙRR
A'GHREADAIDH 2W/RII

Glen Brittle 2 miles 3 furlongs 2,700ft of ascent

This route is only for rock climbers if it is intended to continue directly to the parent summit. The walker/scrambler may visit Sgùrr Eadar da Choire by following Route 11 into Coire na Dorus, then from the base of Eag Dubh a broad rake leads across easily to the neck behind the higher of the two rocky peaklets. To reach Sgùrr a' Ghreadaidh he must retrace his step to Route 11 and climb the North Ridge *(Route 57)*.

A roped team will have better sport by copying Messrs. King, Gibbs and Dobson's exploit of 1898 and taking a climb more or less directly up the north-west ridges and buttresses of Sgùrr Eadar da Choire and Ghreadaidh. This route is open to variation both above and below the twin peaklets and is graded 'Moderate'.

SGÙRR A' MHADAIDH

SGÙRR THUILM   2,885ft.

Route 61   Traverse and W. Ridge of
Mhadaidh   Glen Brittle   4S

SGÙRR A' MHADAIDH   3,012ft

Route 62   South Ridge from An Dorus
                                          Glen Brittle/Coruisk   4S

Route 63   East Ridge   Glen Brittle/Coruisk   RII

Though Sgùrr a' Mhadaidh is the least elevated of the Cuillin's Munros it ranks high in the esteem of all mountaineers who know the Main Ridge well. Another immense block of gabbro occupying a turn in the ridge, it contrasts with its narrow crested neighbour, Ghreadaidh in possessing its best and rockiest face to the north-west rather than the south-east. Also basaltic dykes have severed the mountain into four segments. These revel in the mundane titles of 1st, 2nd, 3rd and 4th tops, that is reading from north-east to south-west, the '4th' being the highest. The gaps between are among the

deepest on the ridge. If sufficient cause is merited to christen any as yet un-named peak in the Cuillin the '1st top' of Mhadaidh must be the leading candidate. Possibly one of the scientist/geologists deserve recognition or would everyone recognise 'Sgùrr na Glaic Moire', I wonder?

Although either end of Mhadaidh may be reached quite easily neither face provides a way for unroped teams, except to mention a ledge on the Coruisk face runs from the base of the gully between the 2nd and 3rd tops on the 600 feet high south face, and traverses up, left and round to reach the Main Ridge between the 3rd top and the summit. Thus an alternative ascent is open to those approaching from Coruisk and Coir' an Uaigneis. The chief glory of Sgùrr a' Mhadaidh however is its north-west face, where rock climbs of up to 1,200 feet of a serious nature are to be found. Included among these is the Foxes Rake, an 'Easy' route, starting from the screes below the Amphitheatre which takes a slanting shelf of rock that debouches onto the North-West Ridge above the col between Thuilm and Mhadaidh, an exposed loose route. The North-West Ridge is that connecting the peak with its only satellite, Sgùrr Thuilm.

The summit of Mhadaidh is a knife-edge with two small cairns 10 yards apart separated by a narrow wall of rock giving shelter from both kinds of exposure.

Nothing higher intervenes between here and Bruach na Frithe 2 miles to the north, therefore a comprehensive view is gained of the northern part of the ridge. The skyline from Bruach to Sgùrr nan Gillean is particularly fine, and the depths of Coruisk impress as greatly as they do from Ghreadaidh.

Descents.   The short south ridge to An Dorus is the more straight-forward way to Glen Brittle. To reach Bealach na Glaic Moire, Coruisk based parties must traverse all the tops of the North-East Ridge. From An Dorus they have An Dorus gully to descend. (*Route 11.*)

SGÙRR THUILM   2,885ft.

The high and shapely cone standing aloof from the Main Ridge is a handy objective for a half day out from the youth hostel in Glen Brittle.

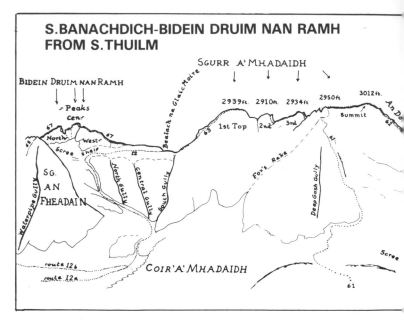

S.BANACHDICH-BIDEIN DRUIM NAN RAMH FROM S.THUILM

61. SGÙRR THUILM AND NORTH-WEST RIDGE.
MHADAIDH 2W/4S

Glen Brittle YH 2 miles 3 furlongs 2,900ft of ascent
(Mhadaidh) 3 miles 1 furlong 3,550ft of ascent

A few outcrops of gabbro half immersed in scree afford little resistance to those making an ascent over Sgùrr Thuilm's western approaches. A rather blunt nose runs down from the top in the hostel's direction. Grass slopes reach well up and offer easy progress from any point on the road through the glen. Scree is encountered at 1,200 feet a mile out from the road, and a buttress is turned on the left at the steepest part of the climb. Beyond this circle to the right with crags falling to the left (north) and scree (right) on the last section of ridge leading to the summit (2 miles 3 furlongs).

Rest and enjoy a fine view of two of the largest corries in Skye - Creiche and Ghreadaidh. If time or conditions necessitate a return an easy safe descent is the route of ascent, the way you came. One can make a descent to Allt a'Choire Ghreadaidh, but a band of cliffs, with

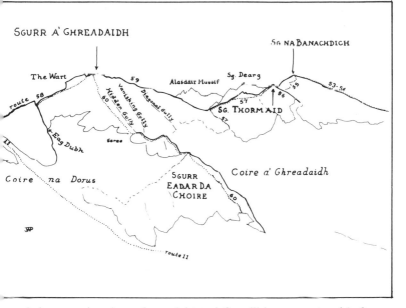

ledges running down from right to left, will be encountered before
the floor of the corrie is reached. The north face of the peak is crag
bound - no way down here.

The East Ridge is a fairly steady descent. The col between Thuilm
and Mhadaidh is a narrow wall of tottery looking rocks. Where these
rocks begin an escape can be made into Coire na Dorus to the south
(right) by dropping 30 feet then continuing horizontally along scree
and grass to open easy ground.

The North-West Ridge to Mhadaidh now rises steeply in a huge
buttress which is rent on the left by a deep corner - Deep Gash Gully.
Exposed slabs (or a gully further right) offer the easiest way, right of
the crest of the ridge and join more buttresses coming in on the left from
the north-west face. Foxes Rake joins our ridge at a small saddle with
a cairn. The rest of the ridge is easy and leads to the north end of
Mhadaidh where the Main Ridge is reached leading up to the right after
a 40 feet chimney. Ledges on the west (right) of the narrow crest lead
in 150 yards to the top.

62. SGÙRR A'MHADAIDH - SOUTH RIDGE from AN DORUS 4S

Glen Brittle YH 2¾ miles 3,050ft of ascent
Coruisk Hut 4 miles 1 furlong 3,050ft of ascent

Having reached An Dorus via Route 11 (2 miles 5 furlongs from Glen Brittle, 4 miles - Coruisk) turn north and follow the scratches along the Main Ridge. The scramble is a good one for scramblers, though ramblers will find it difficult, and danglers do not bother to grade this section at all! No gaps are encountered (if you find one you are on Ghreadaidh!) as you ascend the 250 feet, 170 yards to the summit. The shortest route in the book! From An Dorus a steepish but short scramble to the ridge is made right of the steep rocks. Above a bouldery section avoid more rocks on the left until one is eventually forced onto the crest which though less steep becomes very exposed on the Coruisk side.

63. SGÙRR A' MHADAIDH from BEALACH NA GLAIC MOIRE RII

Glen Brittle Road 3¼ miles 3,350ft of ascent
Coruisk Hut 4 miles 3 furlongs 3,350ft of ascent

This route is strictly for the rock climber. Although graded 'Moderate' in rock climbing guides a great deal of climbing is involved, some of it exposed and certainly not easy to follow in mist. Good conditions and companions must be chosen for this excursion. The ridge is usually taken in the reverse direction to that described, the steeper difficulties lying on the west sides of the tops.

Begin by attaining Bealach na Glaic Moire, 2,492 feet from the road in Glen Brittle (2¾ miles) or the Coruisk Hut (3 miles 7 furlongs). Scrambling begins shortly beyond the Bealach then a steady ascent of 450 feet brings you to the '1st Top' - 2,939 feet. Just beyond, a vertical wall facing Sgùrr a'Ghreadaidh to the south-west, has to be descended. Beyond the gap, 2,858 feet another scramble puts the '2nd Top' 2,910 feet underfoot. A second 50 feet vertical south-west facing wall of rock interrupts the descent to the next gap 2,840 feet. This gap or col is narrow and sensational, overlooking the dizzy precipices of the north-west face through a narrow rift in the rocks falling to Coir' a' Mhadaidh. Another short and steady scramble to the 3rd Top - 2,934 feet precedes a descent to the last gap at 2,820 feet. This descent is easier than those from Tops 1 and 2 and uses more broken rocks on the Coruisk side of the ridge.

From the 2,820 feet 'last' gap Coir' an Uaigneis can be reached via a sloping scree rake running left (facing down) around and down the rocky south face of the 3rd Top. Avoid the gully falling directly below the gap. The rake can be reached from Route 11 by traversing to the right across the flatter portion of Coir' an Uaigneis as far as the bottom of the gully falling from the gap between the 2nd and 3rd Tops.

Meanwhile, back on the Main Ridge, summiteers continue westwards past a pinnacle and a gap to the point where the ridge or buttress from Sgùrr Thuilm joins the Main Ridge. Here the Main Ridge makes an important turn south and soon reaches the 4th and highest top of Sgùrr a' Mhadaidh, ½ mile from Bealach na Glaic Moire.

AN DRUIM NAN RAMH

SGÙRR AN FHEADAIN   2,253ft.

Route 64	South-East approach	Glen Brittle 2W
Route 65	Spur Route	Glen Brittle RI

BIDEIN DRUIM NAN RAMH   2,850ft

Route 66	Ordinary Route Central Peak	Glen Brittle RII
Route 67	Main Ridge Traverse Glen Brittle/Coruisk/ Sligachan	RII

DRUIM NAN RAMH   1,636ft., **DRUIM PINNACLE**   2,467ft.

Route 68	Traverse and continuation to Bidein	2W/RII

MEALLAN DEARG   1,060ft.

Route 69	Ascent from Sligachan or Coruisk	1W

MEALL DEARG   1,196ft.

Route 70	Ascent from Sligachan or Coruisk	1W

DRUIM HAIN   1,141ft.

Route 70	Ascent from Coruisk or Camasunary	1W

SGÙRR HAIN   1,386ft.

Route 71	Ascent from Coruisk	1W

SGÙRR NA STRI   1,631ft.

Route 72	Ascent from Coruisk	2W

The peaks of this Ridge of Oars possesses many satellites. This is a group boasting no Munro. Despite the lack of altitude the culminating point of the range is one of the most difficult to attain even by the easiest route. Bidein is also unique in that two lateral ridges join at the same point on the Main Ridge. The south-eastern of these is by far the longest of all the branches and winds for miles over several lowish humps before terminating in a magnificent fashion in the sea-girt rocky cone of Sgùrr na Stri. Each of these hills has for convenience been described under a separate 'route' number.

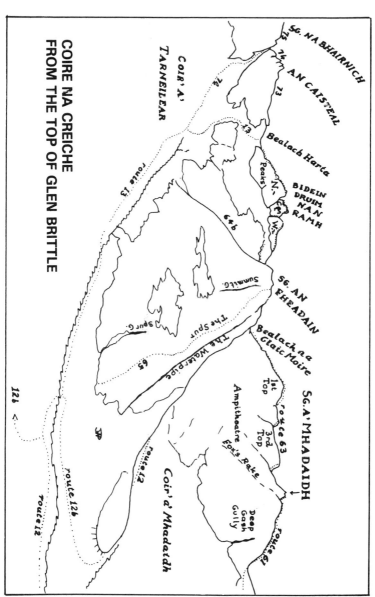

COIRE NA CREICHE
FROM THE TOP OF GLEN BRITTLE

SG. NA BHAIRNICH

AN CAISTEAL

Bealach Harta

BIDEIN
DRUIM
NAN
RAMH

COIR' A'
TARNEILEAR

N. (S.)
Peaks)

W.

route 13

Summit

SG. AN
FHEADAIN

The Spur

Spur G.

Bealach na
Glaic Moire

The Waterpipe

SG. A'MHADAIDH

1st
Top

route 63

3rd
Top

Amphitheatre

Fox's Rake

Deep
Gash
Gully

Coir' a'Mhadaidh

route 12b

route 12

route 61

SGÙRR AN FHEADAIN 2,253ft.

A pointed symmetrical peak steals the scene which is presented to the road bound traveller emerging from the forest en route for Glen Brittle. Around Coire na Creiche, a circle of magnificent peaks provide a golden panorama of rock under evening sunshine. In pride of place, the Peak of the Waterpipe, as Professor Collie called it, steals the show in a most assertive manner even if dwarfed by Mhadaidh and Bidein. The long deep gash which suggested the name of the peak, is one of the longest in the Cuillin and provides rock climbers with a notoriously prolonged and difficult course. Obviously the rocks on either side must also be reserved for the fraternity of the rope, but its summit can be attained by a short and easy scramble from the short 'neck' of the loose rocks connecting Sgùrr an Fheadain to the South Top of Bidein on the Main Ridge and this approach is obviously the best way of descent via the col and Coir' a' Tarneilear.

64. SGÙRR AN FHEADAIN 3S/RII
   from (a) Coir a'Mhadaidh
   from (b) Coir' a'Tarneilear
   Glen Brittle 2 miles 5 furlongs 2,100ft of ascent

(a) Coir' a' Mhadaidh is reached via route 12 to Bealach na Glaic Moire. Instead of taking the scree gully left of the headwall of the corrie guarding the direct approach to the bealach, turn left or north over scree and rock to a col. Otherwise stick to the Bealach route until just below the Main Ridge. Now turn back and left to descend an easy ridge for 150 yards. An easy scramble brings one to the small col at 2,120 feet. The final short climb involves some rock turrets before the top, passable on left.

(b) Coir' a' Tarneilear provides a slightly shorter approach to the col. In clear weather at least the approach is obvious - one simply follows the stream draining that corrie until the rocks on the north flank of your objective are passed on the right. Beyond them a line of screes leads from the headwaters of the stream to the col at 2,120 feet.

A bird's-eye view of the web of streamlets draining the vast bowl provides contrast to the awesome prospect of Sgùrr a' Mhadaidh's precipices.

65. 'THE SPUR' OF SGÙRR AN FHEADAIN RI-II
Glen Brittle 2¼ miles   2,050ft of ascent

The preceding route will be regarded as a 'cheat' by many. Although the route to be described provides the easiest frontal attack it is fairly exposed and is really a rock climb. Steadiness is required as belays are scarce. In 1907 Messrs. Abraham and Harland came this way finding more sporting interest in two gullies which cleave the lower (Spur Gully) and higher (Summit Gully) bands of rock, which they graded 'Moderate'. These can be avoided to the left and right respectively and altogether 1,200 feet of easy climbing on gabbro can be enjoyed, more interestingly as one gains height. Just before the summit the ridge levels and a pinnacle intervenes which is passed on the left.

BIDEIN DRUIM NAN RAMH   2,850ft.

The mountain consists of a complex trio of gabbro peaks standing where two important lateral ridges abut on a bend in the Main Ridge. Approaches can be made from all three centres - Brittle, Coruisk and Sligachan. The highest, Central Peak was reached in autumn 1883 by Lawrence Pilkington, Hulton and Walker. Little rock climbing has been recorded hereabouts.

66. CENTRAL PEAK, BIDEIN DRUIM NAN RAMH- ORDINARY WAY   RII

Glen Brittle Road 2 miles 7 furlongs   2,700ft of ascent
Coruisk 4 miles 1 furlong   2,900ft of ascent
Sligachan via Harta Corrie 7 miles 1 furlong
via Bealach a' Mhaim 5½ miles   2,900ft of ascent

(a)   From Glen Brittle climb the scree shoot left of the slabs below Bealach na Glaic Moire (*Route 12*) then traverse left below the west peak of Bidein 2,779 feet and enter the bouldery gully running up to the gap between the west and central peaks. There is no mistaking one's whereabouts here for a massive boulder, the Bridge Rock, is wedged across the top of the gap. This point can be reached via Coir' a' Tarneilear by traversing under the west face of the north peak.

(b)   From Coruisk head for the summit of Bealach na Glaic Moire (*Route 12)* then turn the west peak on the north by screes as described in (a) above.

(c)   From Sligachan reach Bealach na Glaic Moire via Am Mam

(Route 12) see (a) above. Alternatively Bealach Harta can be ascended from Harta Corrie *(Route 13)*, then the north peak is by-passed over screes to the north-west.

From the Bridge Rock at 2,710 feet rope up and move up and right up rock steps to a 'sentry box'. Turn the overhang on the left on large holds to reach a slab with incut holds. Scree slopes lead to a mini chimney of basalt. Another short wall poses a simple climb then more scree is traversed right to a cracked block guarding a moss carpeted, level but airy summit platform.

67. BIDEIN DRUIM NAN RAMH - MAIN RIDGE TRAVERSE RII

Bealach na Glaic Moire -
Bealach Harta ½ mile 500ft of ascent

Route 12 describes the approaches to Bealach na Glaic Moire. The ascent thence of the West Peak 2,779 feet is a not too difficult scramble. On a broad north facing slab teeters the 'summit' - a cottage sized block. Creep past it on the right, Coruisk side down the exposed steep slab to a final awkward overlap just above the gap in the ridge at 2,710 feet in which is jammed the younger brother of the summit block. This chockstone - the Bridge Rock - reached by routes 66 and 68 is crossed onto the south face of the Central Peak 2,850 feet. Route 66 describes the short climb to its mossy summit.

Do not continue the line taken on the ascent but return over the cracked block, cross scree then follow a trap dyke left (west) of the ridge until it steepens. Descend a slab on the right then climb down a difficult step just to the Coruisk side of a prow. Another dyke runs left of the narrow crest for a short section before the ridge falls away dramatically to the Central/North-east Peak Gap 2,700 feet. A slab is descended half right where a vertical 6 foot corner (avoided further right but where loose blocks make rope handling dangerous) lands one on a narrow step. Move along it left (looking down) towards the gap which is reached down a final awkward overhang. The continuation over the North Top 2,794 feet begins 10 feet above the gap where a ledge leads beneath unclimbable rocks up and left to an easy nose which climbs directly to the lofty overhung end of the summit ridge, 20 yards south-west of the summit cairn. Bealach Harta 300 feet below is reached down pleasant slabs keeping just right of the crest with 3 platforms breaking the continuity of the rock. A ledge on the left side looks easy but crosses a steep slaggy flank and is not recommended as the finish of this entertaining traverse, over one of the more complicated sections of the Main Ridge.

68. BIDEIN via DRUIM NAN RAMH RII/2W

Coruisk Hut 4 miles 3,300ft of ascent
Sligachan 7 miles 1 furlong 3,000ft of ascent

An excellent excursion to make during the first day of a prolonged stay at the Coruisk Hut, or Sligachan, for no other could display so much of the topography of the Black Cuillin in as much mileage. All incursions from Sligachan onto the ridge are mentioned below. Start the day from Coruisk taking the stepping stones across the short lived River Scavaig. Rounding the eastern shore of Loch Coruisk cross the Coire Riabhaich Burn to the base of the gabbro rocks at the south-east extremity of the ice worn Ridge of Oars. This long arm of high ground boasts a continuous precipice on its Coruisk flank over the whole of its 3 miles. Anyone considering an alternative route back on that side should decline any descent in that direction. From east to west an almost unbroken series of slabs are succeeded by immense buttresses which harbour 1,000 feet Severe rock climbs. Many grass ledges and rakes abound further west. No continuously easy or straightforward route is suitable for walking parties. Returning to the beginning (or end) of our ridge one is confronted with steep holdless gabbro dipping into the grass at hardly 200 feet above sea level. A direct approach involves 'Difficult' rock work but away round to the right or north a burn can be followed to a break in the rocks guarding the ridge. On its broad back easy walking over slabs of gabbro dotted with small pools, brings one to the barely distinguishable summit at 1,636 feet, of Druim nan Ramh (1 mile 7 furlongs).

The way to Sligachan hence would be due north across the plateau for 5-600 yards until the rock falls away steeply. Traverse left along this edge, then follow a break in the rock running slightly left northwest and down until the slope relents. Below, a burn will lead to the Sligachan River ¾ mile above the Bloody Stone 2 miles 5 furlongs from the summit.

Continuing beyond the summit, the plateau narrows gradually as we proceed over undulating ground. The views of the Central Cuillin are superb on a fine day. In mist, navigation would be tricky until the ridge takes an appreciable rise of 600 feet beyond a good mile of level going. Two pools lie close to each other at the bottom of the rise. Down the north side of the ridge a convenient rake descends in a north-east direction to Harta Corrie and, similarly, an easy gully runs east to the same corrie from just before the top of the 600 feet rise at 2,125 feet. The ridge becomes rougher as one advances to a drop where a basalt dyke crosses our path. Turn the drop on the left (south) side and cross the stony flanks of the spectacular Druim Pinnacle 2,476 feet (3¾ miles). This knife-edged peak is unnamed in recent literature but Ashley Abraham referred to it in his publication of 1908. A knife-edge worthy of some title, it is only climbable on its southern face (RI), the ends being overhanging shaky rock. A hundred yard stony level section of ridge beyond is abruptly terminated by the gigantic, partly overhanging south-east wall of the Central Peak. No one has reciprocated the remarkable descent (on a doubled rope by a Doctor Lütscher in the 1920's) of this precipice. We can, however, follow in the wake of the pioneer party of 1883. A nasty but loose and grassy ledge leads us left across the steep south-west face to the gap and Bridge Rock between the West and Central Peaks, whence Route 66 leads to the Summit of Bidein in two steep pitches. Another way to the mossiest summit in the Cuillin, avoiding the loose ledge, is to climb rocks above the ledge to another higher one that rises gradually towards the east end of the summit.

From the gap between the Druim Pinnacle and the Central Peak, a steep scree gully runs down to Harta Corrie. After a loss of 300 feet the fell side opens out. Continue straight down to a corridor of easy ground between extensive slabs overlooking the upper bowl of Harta Corrie. From Bidein's Central Peak to the Bloody Stone by this gully is about 2½ miles.

69. MEALLAN DEARG 1,060ft. 1W
Coruisk Hut 2¾ miles, Sligachan 5¼ miles

The Red Hills are composed of a narrow belt of volcanic rocks running across the Sligachan River west of the Bloody Stone to the upper hollow of Coire Riabhach. The highest point stands central to these rocks which have been intruded into the gabbro. The whole area is somewhat undulating and it would be difficult to find the actual 1,060ft point in mist.

Coruisk Cross the Scavaig by the stepping stones and ascend Coire Riabhach. A mile beyond the loch, the rock knoll lies right of some pools lying in the last hollow before the steeper descent into Harta Corrie to the north. A simple walk up the 200 feet western slope brings one to the top.

Sligachan. The pools mentioned above can be reached via the Bloody Stone 4¾ miles: see *Routes 2 and 13.* South of the Stone an escarpment of gabbro cliffs is seen. Walk along the south bank of the Sligachan River to a point immediately below the right or western extremity of the cliffs and climb the slope to the summit beyond.

Access to Meall Dearg and Druim Hain is a simple stroll over the lochan studded moorland.

70. MEALL DEARG 1,196ft. IW
Coruisk Hut 3 miles, Sligachan 5 miles
Camasunary 4¼ miles

DRUIM HAIN 1,141ft 1W
Coruisk Hut 2½ miles, Sligachan 5½ miles
Camasunary 4¼ miles

The Red Hill, the only granite peak described, stands more assertively than its neighbours, overlooking the junction of the Glen of Sligachan and Srath na Crèitheach. A 300ft band of granophyre guards the north. Druim Hain is a broad, indistinctive, pooly ridge. The cairned top lies a quarter-mile south of Meall Dearg. On some maps it is spelt Druim an Eidhne.

Descents by routes described are simple and safe but remember the cliffs above Sligachan Glen.

From Sligachan follow Route 2 and 13 to the Bloody Stone (4¾ miles). Forge on 100 yards to the next burn flowing into the Sligachan River. Turn left and follow it to a tarn on the plateau above a line of slabs. For Meall Dearg turn left and ascend the final 200 feet over grass and scree to the round top. For Druim Hain carry on due south for a further 500 yards.

From Camasunary follow Route 3 to Loch an Athain (3 miles) cross the river flowing into the loch. Ascend bouldery slopes, crossing the Coruisk - Sligachan path en route. Druim Hain lies beyond the top of the hollow section of the wall, and Meall Dearg lies well to the right.

From Coruisk follow the Sligachan path Route 2 to the top of the pass between Druim Hain and Sgùrr na Stri. (1½ miles). Follow the broad ridge on the left for a mile past small pools and cross over Druim Hain and circle gradually right to Meall Dearg 500 yards beyond.

71. SGÙRR HAIN   1,386ft.   1W

Coruisk hut 1¾ miles, Camasunary 2 miles,
Sligachan 6½ miles

This hill boasts a 400 feet gabbro cliff on its east face overlooking Loch na Crèitheach. No climbing has been recorded here. On the west flank overlooking Route 2 stands Captain Maryon's Cairn.

From Camasunary cross the footbridge and follow the true right bank of the river to a bend at ½ mile. Continue up the tributary draining the basin ahead. The right-hand slopes form the southern rim of Sgùrr Hain's summit plateau. The south top at 1,377 feet lies 200 yards beyond and 500 yards further is the narrower higher north summit.

From Coruisk travellers bound for Sligachan on Route 2 can deviate onto the broad simple ridge walk of 400 yards south south-east from the top of the pass. On the west flank of Sgùrr Hain stands a 8½ feet tall pyramid of stones marking the final resting place of a missing lone excursionist, one Captain Maryon. It was the custom in Skye for such cairns to be erected by people who kept their identity secret. This 6 ton example was engineered by a single devoted and strong friend.

72. SGÙRR NA STRI   1,631ft.   2W

Coruisk Hut 1½ miles, Camasunary 2 miles
Sligachan 10 miles

Despite its lack of stature, this Peak of Strife, also known as Sgùrr Strudhidh or Trondhu, is one of Scotland's better known eminences. Though it is rarely ascended, it figures prominently in the calendar picture postcard view of the Cuillin from Elgol. However, its chief merit must be the superb panorama obtained at the summit. Lochs Coruisk and Scavaig play the starring roles in a galaxy of talent on display in every direction. C.R.Weld who made the first tourist ascent in 1859, challenged his fellow Alpine Club members with the myriad and difficult, indeed, inaccessible peaks he beheld from the 'peak of strife'.

The twin summits have the sea on two sides and are almost encircled by slabs of gabbro. On the west they fall to the very shores of Loch Scavaig and provide unspecified climbing routes. An open gully runs from between the summits due south. It might provide a feasible way from Rubha Bàn, but for the walker (and Mr Weld) the route to the top is rather Hobson's Choice - the North Ridge.

From Sligachan attain the top of the pass over Druim Hain on Route 2, then traverse Sgùrr Hain and continue south over a broadening depression.

From Coruisk the depression is reached easily over simple slopes from the vicinity of Loch a' Choire Riabhaich on Route 2. Captain Maryon's monument may be inspected on the way.

The start of the North Ridge can also be reached from Camasunary. Cross the footbridge and go up the west bank for half a mile before taking the tributary draining the corrie ahead and left. Turn the cliffs on the right where they dwindle to a gap in some rocks and, just beyond is the beginning of the broad North Ridge.

AN CAISTEAL   2,724ft
Route 73   South Ridge   Glen Brittle/Sligachan 4S
Route 74   North Ridge   Glen Brittle RI

SGÙRR NA BHAIRNICH   2,826ft
Route 75   Traverse and South Ridge   Bruach na Frithe 4S

BRUACH NA FRITHE   3,143ft
Route 76   From Fionn Choire Sligachan/Glen Brittle 2W
Route 77   North-west Ridge   Sligachan/Glen Brittle 3S

SGÙRR A' FIONN CHOIRE   3,068ft
Route 78   North Face   Sligachan 3S/4S

BRUACH NA FRITHE

Bruach na Frithe is reputed to be the easiest summit of the Cuillin, though nothing could be simpler than the walk up the West Ridge of Sgùrr na Banachdich. The three ridges of Bruach, however, offer little resistance to a walker. The northern face below is written off as easy by climbing guides but crags are encountered below the North-West Ridge. The western and eastern facets are steep and loose with extensive rock outcrops rendering routes dangerous as well as uncomfortable and fatiguing. The satellites of Sgùrr na Bhairnich and An Caisteal are more solidly constructed with huge gabbro slabs falling for up to 1,000 feet on either side of the Main Ridge while Sgùrr a' Fionn Choire is an enormous wedge of gabbro surrounded by screes.

AN CAISTEAL   2,724ft.

The terrain here as elsewhere consists of outward sloping slabs and overlaps on the Coruisk side and ledges on the Tarneilear side. Some climbs of 'Very Difficult' and harder standards have been made on the slabby flank of this mountain by Harold Raeburn and others in the early years of this century after being repulsed by the gullies which split them. These gullies are still unclimbed. The western rocks have no routes described in climbing guides. The peak was christened by Professor Harker.

Descents. A choice here. A competent party in a hurry will make the shorter but more awkward descent to the north col, (*Route 74*) then take the scree slope west into Coir' a' Tarneilear, though others may prefer the longer but more complicated South Ridge, (*Route 73*). Remember Sligachan is easily reached from Coir' a' Tarneilear via Bealach a'Mhaim. Any route into Harta Corrie will be more difficult and (unexpectedly) further to Sligachan.

Harta Corrie is seen to advantage from the summit, but the skyline to the north will hold most attention.

73. AN CAISTEAL VIA SOUTH RIDGE 4S

Sligachan 6 miles 5 furlongs 3,300ft of ascent
Glen Brittle 2 ¼ miles 2,850ft of ascent

Attain Bealach Harta 2,498ft via Route 13. The way north commences with a short steep wall to a level, easy section of the Main Ridge. After a couple of hundred yards two narrow gaps or slits are encountered where basaltic dykes crossing the ridge have weathered. One of them constitutes a 'bad step' where a brave stride takes one over the void. A pinnacle hereabouts may be turned on the left. A further 150 yards of scrambling brings one to the summit a quarter mile from the bealach.

74. AN CAISTEAL VIA NORTH RIDGE RI

Sligachan 6½ miles 3,250ft of ascent
Glen Brittle 2 miles 5 furlongs 2,850ft of ascent

Route 13 is followed into Coir' a' Tarneilear. Instead of bearing right (south) take the continuous scree-shoot falling directly from the Caisteal-Bhairnich col, 2,507 feet. This point *can* be reached by rock climbers from Lota Corrie by crossing a rock wall onto the easy upper part of the gully falling from the 2,507 col at a point overlooking the wet abyss dropping into Harta Corrie.

From the col one is confronted on the south by a steep almost overhanging wall. The well worn route climbs this directly for 20 to 30 feet. Trend right to easier rocks on the Tarneilear side then attain the ridge where a steep nose will be encountered. This difficulty can be turned on the left or east before moving back onto the crest of a final ridge.

SGÙRR NA BHAIRNICH   2,826ft.

This peak was also unnamed until Professor Harker found a title for it. No climbing has been recorded on the mountain although it is almost composed entirely of bare gabbro on its culminating 800 feet. The top affords a bird's-eye view of Lota Corrie.

Descents. For Sligachan, traverse Bruach na Frithe and descend the Fionn Choire (*Route 76*). The South Ridge and the scree run to Coir' a' Tarneilear and Route 13 will see you to Glen Brittle.

75.   TRAVERSE OF SGÙRR NA BHAIRNICH AND SOUTH RIDGE OF BRUACH NA FRITHE   4S

Glen Brittle 3¼ miles 3,200ft of ascent
Sligachan 5½ miles 3,400ft of ascent

The col south of Sgùrr na Bhairnich at 2,507 feet can be reached via Routes 13 and 74 (2¾ and 5 miles). Above the col scramble to a pinnacle south-west of Sgùrr na Bhairnich's summit over loose scree then loose, stepped rock. At the gap behind the pinnacle turn overhangs on the right without losing much height to turn a wall beyond.

Beyond the summit scramble down to the gap at 2,772 feet and an easy promenade up a broad ridge. A scree-filled gap graced by a boulder is followed by a short scramble up a corner on the right. A few rocks are found just short of the summit of Bruach na Frithe.

BRUACH NA FRITHE   3,143ft.

The 'easy peak' of the Cuillin received its first recorded visit in May 1845 when Professor Forbes, the pioneering scientist, placed a barometer on the summit and recorded a height not far above that given by modern maps. The north face has some large but broken cliffs. The west face consists of steep scree and discontinuous but extensive bands of steep cliffs and should be avoided. The south-east face is similar. The summit lies at a sharp turn on the Main Ridge on the junction of three ridges and must be the easiest to identify, sporting the only triangulation pillar on the Main Ridge. Visitors new to the Highlands will be intrigued by its cylindrical pattern.

The view is one of the most celebrated in Scotland. The curves on the Main Ridge are more apparent seen from here than elsewhere.

Descents.   For Sligachan, the East Ridge and Fionn Choire provide a comfortable and rapid way. For Glen Brittle, the East Ridge for

Fionn Choire or North-west Ridge and Bealach a' Mhaim offer reliable if circuitous descents. Lóta Corrie can be best reached by the col to the east, but habitation in that direction is nil.

76. BRUACH NA FRITHE VIA FIONN CHOIRE 2W

Sligachan 4 miles 3 furlongs   3,200ft of ascent
Glen Brittle Road 3 miles 3 furlongs   3,000 ft of ascent

The col 2,964 feet 250 yards east of the summit can be reached from Route 14 by eschewing either approach to Bealach nan Lice at the base of the rocks of Sgùrr a' Fionn Choire and turning that peak to the west i.e. left on the Fionn Choire approach.

The East Ridge is the simplest of walks taking a rise of 200 feet along the way.

77. BRUACH NA FRITHE - NORTH-WEST RIDGE 3S

Sligachan 4¼ miles 3,200ft of ascent
Glen Brittle Road 3¼ miles 2,950ft of ascent

This ridge provides the most entertaining way up the mountain and nowhere demands too much strain. Recommended for a first day out or to those with little time at their disposal.

The path described in *Route 1* to Bealach a' Mhàim is easy to follow. Glen Brittle Road 1 mile 7 furlongs/Sligachan 3 miles. From the Màm (as the pass was called) head south over short grass and take the crest of the blunt ridge. At a quarter of a mile a 'false' top - Sròn Tobar nan Uais-lean 1,682 feet is reached. Beyond, the ridge climbs less steeply for a while. A mile from the Màm another vague ridge or shoulder joins ours from the left, distinguished by a line of cairns widely spaced leading to Route 14, and providing a more direct way to Sligachan. The ridge narrows and becomes rougher with cliffs developing at either hand. No difficulties occur if the crest is adhered to. Another level stretch, 2,580 feet, precedes the most imposing section. If you wish, stay with the crest and some scrambling will be enjoyed, but if the rocks are greasy an easy rake can be used 100 feet below the crest on the right, or west flank. On the other, Fionn Choire side, high cliffs fall from the ridge. Rejoin the ridge as soon as you are able as further traversing will take you onto a steep loose slope with rocks above and below. The upper section of the ridge reverts to an easy walk before the summit is reached.

SGÙRR A' FIONN CHOIRE   3,068ft.

As this top lies between rather illustrious neighbours it is rather forgotten. On its usual (northern) approach water is available from a mossy spring 200 feet below Bealach nan Lice. At 2,700 feet the Cuillin's highest 'tap'. Perched on the top one experiences satisfaction on two counts. Firstly the peak provides a good scramble and as a bonus the view of its neighbours is excellent. The quickest way to Sligachan is down Route 14. Those bound for Glen Brittle may cross Bruach na Frithe and descend the North-west Ridge to the Màm Route 1   2 miles 3 furlongs.

78.   SGÙRR A' FIONN CHOIRE
NORTH-WEST RIDGE/NORTH GULLY   4/3S

Sligachan 4¼ miles   3,100ft of ascent
Glen Brittle Road 3 miles 3 furlongs   2,900ft of ascent

The summit rocks are surrounded by scree and two easy passes or gaps on the Main Ridge give access to the north-west and east at the 2,964 feet col and Bealach nan Lice respectively. These approaches are described in Route 14. A long buttress falls from the summit into Lota Corrie. Its 600 feet overlapping slabs are reserved for the hardman. The 'West Ridge' gives a short scramble from the 2,964ft col with an awkward 20 feet nose providing the crux. North of the summit two corners or gullies provide 100 feet simple scrambles and serve as the easiest approach and descent. East of the top, huge overlaps preclude a super-direct way.

AM BÀSTEIR

SGÙRR A' BHÀSTEIR   2,951ft

Route 79	South Ridge	Sligachan 2W
Route 80	North-East Ridge	Sligachan 3S

MEALL ODHAR   2,085ft.

Route 81	Traverse and North West Ridge of Sgùrr a' Bhàsteir	2W/3S

BASTEIR TOOTH   3,005ft.

Route 82	Collie's Ordinary Route	Sligachan RIII
Route 83	Naismith's Route	RIV

AM BÀSTEIR   3,069ft.

Route 84	East Ridge	Sligachan RI
Route 85	West Ridge from Tooth	RIII

The Executioner group comprises a remarkable trio of gabbro peaks. Although completely encircled and intersected by simple scree slopes they offer the greatest difficulty even to rock climbers. The Tooth is the *pièce de resistance* of the whole range being the most difficult 3,000 feet top in Britain. Its appearance is both awe-inspiring and off putting. The natives gave the parent mountain the title Sgùrr Dubh a' Bhàsteir meaning Black Peak of the Executioner, due no doubt to the Tooth's resemblance to that instrument of death associated with bygone ages. Today ropeless climbers should heed the implications of the present day phrase of 'The Chop' when venturing onto the Tooth. Am Bàsteir can also claim inaccessibility for unroped walkers but the outlying Sgùrr to the north is approachable and affords the finest viewpoint on this end of the Cuillin.

SGÙRR A' BHÀSTEIR   2,951ft.

A shapely cone of gabbro, this peak is often mistaken for Bruach na Frithe when seen from the Sligachan direction, hardly flattery as it is shapelier and boasts more rock than Bruach. If it over-topped the 3,000 feet level its fame would be assured. The three faces are nearly all rock broken by grass and some scree ledges. Two ridges give excellent scrambles while the South Ridge gives the only easy though delightful route to the summit. No climbing has been recorded apart from a naked foray by Alpine Club members up the Bhasteir Gorge at the foot of the mountain in 1890. The satellite Meall Odhar 2,085 feet is relatively tame, boasting only a line of low cliffs west of its top.

Pride of place in the panorama goes unreservedly to Sgùrr nan Gillean. The western flank of the beautiful Pinnacle Ridge is a classic scene and will never be forgotten by whoever finds himself on this small pointed summit on a fine, clear day. Northwards the Trotternish Heights and the Storr rocks may be seen. The easiest way down is the South Ridge to Route 14.

79. SGÙRR A' BHÀSTEIR SOUTH RIDGE   2W

Sligachan 4½ miles   3,000ft of ascent
Glen Brittle Road 3½ miles   2,800ft of ascent

Bealach nan Lice and another saddle 2,848 feet north of the Tooth are both easily reached over scree from either Fionn Choire or Coire a' Bhasteir. It should be noted however, a vertical wall of rock runs due west from the Tooth and peters out at Bealach nan Lice. It faces north. From the Bealach (*Route 14*) a narrowing shattered ridge leads gently down to 2,848 feet then equally gently up to the top. This narrow 300 yard crest is easy but exhilerating.

80. SGÙRR A' BHÀSTEIR - NORTH-EAST RIDGE   3S

Sligachan 3 miles 3 furlongs   3,000ft of ascent

The North-east Ridge is reached from the path up Coire a' Bhasteir beyond the steep section above the gorge (*Route 15*). Optional scrambling is encountered. Some exciting views of Lochain a' Bhàsteir down steep gullies on the left will be found on the ascent. Scree slopes make the last 200 feet easier.

81. MEALL ODHAR AND SGÙRR A' BHÀSTEIR NORTH-WEST RIDGE   2W/3S

Sligachan 3 miles 3 furlongs   3,000ft of ascent

Meall Odhar can be ascended from all directions, though odd crags occur around the top. The most continuous occur in a low line west of, and just below the top.

From Glen Brittle take Route 1 to the Màm, then cross laboriously a mile wide hillside below Fionn Choire to the neck just south of the top of Meall Odhar 2,038 feet.

From Sligachan follow the path up the Allt Dearg Beag *(Route 15)* to a stony, open hollow short of the Bhasteir Gorge. Head south-west up this depression over grass and scree to the neck, 2,038 feet just south of Meall Odhar. On the right a hundred yards distant lies the summit of Meall Odhar.

To continue to Sgùrr a' Bhasteir return across the col along a wide ridge to the base of the rock triangle of the mountain. The initial rocks are avoided on the left where more broken ground provides an easier way. Beyond, the ridge provides a good and interesting scramble. Higher up, the rocks become more shattered and easier before the summit is reached.

BASTEIR TOOTH   3,005ft.

Unclimbed until 1889, the tooth cannot be entertained by non-rock climbers. Those following the ridge at this point should by-pass the problem. Begin the detour at Bealach nan Lice and follow the base of a low but vertical cliff forming a wall north of the Main Ridge between the Bealach and the Tooth. The top of the wall abuts on the Tooth and walkers following the crest must retrace their steps.

Turn Am Bàsteir and the Tooth along the base of the immense brooding overhangs of their north faces. In passing, take note of the 'Very Difficult' and subterranean King's Cave-a deep chimney leading to the Nick between the Tooth and Am Bàsteir. 200 feet of re-ascent leads to Bealach a' Bhàsteir east of Am Bàsteir, the parent peak beyond the Tooth on this quarter mile 'detour'. About 400 feet of re-ascent is required going west. A similar diversion is possible to the south of the peaks over the screes on the 'sunny side' but the track to the north is continuous and less height is lost.

Descents from the top are normally affected by abseil. The most expedient way off is the descent to the Nick then up the western wall of Am Basteir to that summit and its east ridge.

82. BASTEIR TOOTH
ORDINARY ROUTE (COLLIE'S)   RIII

Sligachan 3 miles 6 furlongs Bhasteir Gorge 4 ¼ miles
Fionne Choire   3,050ft of ascent

This the 'easiest' way up the Tooth is a 'Difficult' and very steep rock climb of about 400 feet. Graded as 'Moderate' in early rock climbing guides and unchanged. The ascent is begun from the top of the screes on the south side of the mountain. The Nick between the

113

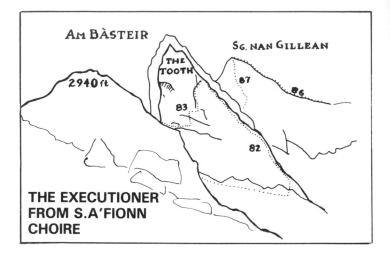

AM BÀSTEIR

THE TOOTH

2940 ft

SG. NAN GILLEAN

87

86

83

82

THE EXECUTIONER FROM S.A'FIONN CHOIRE

Tooth and Am Basteir is attained via a steep open corner beneath. From the Nick go left up easy inclined rock to the airy summit. This is the original route to the summit made by Collie and MacKenzie.

83. BASTEIR TOOTH
SOUTH-WEST FACE (NAISMITH'S) RIV
Sligachan 3 miles 3 furlongs   3,050ft of ascent

A direct 'Very Difficult' or 'Severe' way can be made by rock climbing parties from Bealach nan Lice to the top of the Tooth up the south-west face. This climb was pioneered by Naismith and Mackay in 1898. It is extremely steep and exposed. Its appearance will certainly put off any inexperienced parties. From the Bealach follow the crest of the rock ridge. Where the ridge abuts on the Tooth, descend a few feet to a horizontal terrace crossing the north face, follow this for 30-40 feet to an easy corner. Climb this to a wider terrace which dwindles to a ledge on the right. Almost at the end of the ledge a steep and smooth shallow corner gives access to a chimney 20 feet up and to its left. The chimney is easy but exposed. 15 feet from the top it becomes a thin crack. A slanting crack to the right is followed to the sloping 'roof' of the Tooth.

AM BÀSTEIR   3.069ft.

The north face of the Executioner is a steep 400 feet overhang. The south face is also steep, but unlike the other has no climbers' routes. The summit is quite airy being poised over 'nothing' to north and west. The depths of Coire a' Bhàsteir are impressive.

The 'Moderate' East Ridge is the safest way down.

84.   AM BÀSTEIR - EAST RIDGE   RI
Sligachan 3 miles 3 furlongs   3,100ft of ascent

The Bealach a' Bhàsteir, Route 15, approach serves as the easiest way of climbing the peak. The ridge is a simple rock climb which is quite exposed. The 300-yard ridge begins with a walk. Difficulties are turned on the right (north). A short descent occurs half-way along the loose crest.

85.   AM BÀSTEIR, WEST APPROACH FROM THE TOOTH   RIII
70 yards 250ft of ascent

This climb will usually be made in conjunction with an ascent of the Tooth. From the Nick go right (south) over easy rock to a loose corner which one ascends on the left. A small very steep chimney finishes the climbing. This route is graded 'Difficult' and open to variation.

Walking parties going between Bruach na Frithe and Sgùrr nan Gillean will be obliged to leave the Main Ridge. *See under Basteir Tooth above.*

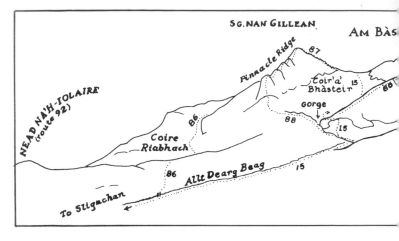

SGURR NAN GILLEAN GROUP

SGÙRR NAN GILLEAN   3,167ft.

Route 86	'Tourist Route' - S.E. Ridge	Sligachan	4S
Route 87	West Ridge	Sligachan	RII
Route 88	Pinnacle Ridge	Sligachan	RIII

SGÙRR BEAG   2,511ft.

| Route 89 | North Ridge | Sligachan | 2W |
| Route 90 | South Ridge | Sligachan | 2W |

SGÙRR NA H-UAMHA   2,416ft.

| Route 91 | North Ridge | Sligachan | RII |

NEAD NA' H-IOLAIRE   760ft.

| Route 92 | | Sligachan | 2W |

Sgùrr nan Gillean is the Cuillin's best known peak and is ascended often. It is reputed to be the most difficult 'tourist' mountain in Scotland and indeed lives have been lost here. Considered the highest by the pioneers it now ranks as 5th of the Cuillin. Professor Forbes, one of the first climbers to visit the island, made the earliest ascent in 1836, guided by Duncan MacIntyre, a local forester who had been

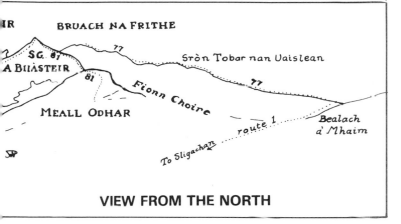

IR   BRUACH NA FRITHE

SG. 87   77   Sròn Tobar nan Uaislean

A BHÀSTEIR   81

Fionn Choire

MEALL ODHAR   77

route 1   Bealach
a' Mhaim

To Sligachan

SP

VIEW FROM THE NORTH

involved in previous attempts. 'The extreme roughness ... rendering the ascent safe.... I have never seen a rock so adapted for clambering.' He followed the South East Ridge which is now known as the Tourist Route. The mountain has two other well defined ridges - The Western, a very narrow affair - and the North. This is the famous Pinnacle Ridge comprising four summits. Both these approaches are reserved for the rock climbers. The south face consists of steep scree and continuous bands of rocks and has been left alone since 1845. The west flank is composed of many buttresses and gullies where the rock climber has a choice of numerous routes of up to 500 feet. A steep band of scree lies beneath this Pinnacle Face and a lower band of rock reaches down to Loch a' Bhasteir. The rocky east face of the Pinnacle Ridge should also be avoided by the walker.

The summit platform is small and airy. The view, of course, is very extensive and interesting in every direction. Knight's Peak is close at hand. The heights and coastline of Trotternish lay far to the north. Eastwards are the Red Cuillin, Glamaig and Marsco. Blaven lies to the south of these cones while the remainder of the arc is occupied by the skyline of the Main Ridge.

Descents. The South-east Ridge is the only feasible way of returning to Sligachan, the well marked path once gained being a sure and safe way home, though climbers having climbed the Pinnacle Ridge traditionally descend the West Ridge to complete a

117

classic day's mountaineering.

86. SGÙRR NAN GILLEAN TOURIST ROUTE - SOUTH-EAST RIDGE 4S
Sligachan 3½ miles   3,250ft of ascent

Begin this much frequented route at Sligachan west of the hotel where a section of obsolete road is used as a lay-by. From the top of the bank on the opposite side of the main road find the path that crosses peat and heather to the footbridge spanning the Red Burn just upstream from the remains of the shed that housed the 'power station'. Cross the bridge and continue over the marshy expanse along a path which gradually climbing joins the left (west) bank of the Allt Dearg Beag. 100 yards after joining the stream cross another footbridge (1 mile 3 furlongs) and continue south along a well defined path that crosses a low moor to Coire Riabhach. This shallow hollow is crossed well right (west) of the lochan. Ahead will be seen a scree-shoot breaking the continuity of the rocks walling the corrie to west and south. This shoot (2½ miles) takes one steeply but suddenly onto a broad bouldery shelf between extensive cliffs on the eastern side of Pinnacle Ridge once known as Coire nan Allt Geala. The well cairned path closes in on the base of the rocks on the right and climbs over scree to a line of easy rock. A terrace running back left overcomes this obstacle and the path zig-zags up a second bouldery hollow to reach the South-east Ridge at 2,600 feet, 300 yards down from the very summit. The first part of the ridge is straightforward but the last hundred yards fetch the hands from everybody's pockets. Short pitches, never very high, require the odd pull up. The first can be avoided but near the top everything has to be taken direct. A basalt dyke on the Harta (south) face runs below the rock steps of the ridge but in the end it peters out some 40 feet below the top, which is reached by a steep scramble.

87. SGÙRR NAN GILLEAN - WEST RIDGE RII
Sligachan 3½ miles   3,200ft of ascent

Reach Bealach a' Bhàsteir via Route 15. Turn left (east) and follow the ridge until a vertical step is encountered. The crest can be reached by a 40ft chimney on the north. However, the famous and entertaining 'Gendarme' or Policeman collapsed in 1987 during rock falls which rendered this section of alarmingly narrow ridge both loose and dangerous. The safest course is to continue over scree on the Coire a' Bhàsteir slope for 200 yards and take the well-worn original route of Nicolson's Chimney - a Moderately graded 'shelf', to gain the crest where the narrow ridge steepens. This section on which difficulties and pinnacles may be turned on the left, constitutes the greater part of the 500 feet ascent which ends in sight of the summit through a hole in the rocks on the left of the ridge.

88. SGÙRR NAN GILLEAN
NORTH OR PINNACLE RIDGE RIII

Sligachan 3 miles 3 furlongs   3,450ft of ascent

The celebrated pinnacles which form the northern ridge of this popular mountain provide one of the best rock climbing courses in Britain. The descent often forms a last lap of an expert's Main Ridge traverse! Its ascent, first made by Charles and Lawrence Pilkington in 1880, always begins at Sligachan where the ridge is only seen end on and the newcomer could hardly suspect the existence of so many independent summits. None the less the Pinnacles make one of the more spectacular mountain scenes when viewed in the late afternoon by a climber perched on the summit of Sgùrr a' Bhàsteir.

The western faces, seen to great advantage from that position, provide many and varied rock climbing routes and were to Sligachan what Sròn na Ciche has become to Glen Brittle - a popular area, concentrated with good climbing. The gullies between the 1st and 2nd, and the 4th and 5th, form the only easy routes. No climbing has been recorded on the discontinuous eastern faces of the pinnacles except the first - the lowest and most northerly. On its northern face two gullies, one above the other, have severities in store for the climber.

The simplest way to reach the base of the First Pinnacle is to take Route 15 to where the Bhasteir Gorge debouches the waters of Allt Dearg Beag. Cross that burn hereabouts at a convenient point opposite a scree slope which leads onto the flattish start of the Pinnacle Ridge. Turn right (south) and walk along the ridge with Coire Riabhach far below on the left and the gorge on the right. 2

miles 5 furlongs, 600 yards steady walking remain before the climbing begins.

Begin on the right or Bhàsteir side where the rocks are broken and give a choice of line. More difficulties will be encountered to the left on the 300 foot climb. From the top of the First Pinnacle (3 miles) at a little over 2,500 feet, little height is lost before another scramble of a hundred feet brings the Second Pinnacle underfoot, 2,655 feet. Again the lowest point is just beyond and hardly any lower. The next ascent is another scramble. Broken rocks lead to a shallow gully which takes you within reach of the sharp splintery summit of the Third Pinnacle at 2,892 feet. This time the ridge drops steeply and reaching the next gap is the hardest and most sensational part of the climb.

Follow the crest going left almost to its end. From it a well-scratched chimney leads down right. This 25 feet section ends on a narrow ledge leading round to the open gully below the summit. Below easier scrambling leads to the main gap, 2,810 feet. It is usual for climbers to abseil this step.

The usual way up Knight's Peak bears to the right for 50 feet along an outward sloping ledge from which easy rocks lead to the summit, 2,994 feet. This peak was first set underfoot in 1873 by another professor - W. Knight who was accompanied by the obligatory guide - a reluctant native named MacPherson. This point had been known variously as the Needle and the Little Horn, then in more modern and less imaginative times as the Fourth Pinnacle.

Like the last, the next descent is about 100 feet, but this time the rocks are more straightforward to another scree ledge at 2,875 feet. A level ridge runs towards the '5th Pinnacle' - Sgùrr nan Gillean itself. Follow this for a few feet then descend on the right down steep rock on good holds until a short gully is reached leading to the foot of the peak. A minor pinnacle stands before the final climb. This is turned on the right. The beginning of the final section is awkward then easier rocks are climbed for 200 feet onto the West Ridge just below the summit.

SGÙRR BEAG 2,511ft.

Sgùrr an Fhithich (Peak of the Raven) was an earlier name for this undistinguished summit, little more than an incident on the way along the long, easy though pleasant ridge linking Sgùrr nan Gillean to its southern outpost, Sgùrr na h-Uamha. Sgùrr Beag's gabbro

120

Sg.na-h-Uamha and Sg.na Stri from Sg. nan Gillean

harbours no routes for the rock climbers. Its rocky eastern spur may give a climb.

Descents. Either route has its snags. Thick mist may cause difficulty for strangers finding the beginning of the 'Tourist Route'. The An Glas-choire route is simple but heavy rain will make a crossing of the Sligachan River dangerous. In fine weather the Tourist Route is the rapid way down.

89. SGÙRR BEAG - NORTH RIDGE 2W

Sligachan 3 miles 7 furlongs 2,700ft of ascent

The summit of Sgùrr Beag is guarded on the Lota Corrie and Sligachan Glen faces by some gabbro walls, but is easily reached from the Tourist Route when that path reaches the South-East Ridge of Sgùrr nan Gillean 3½ miles. (See *Route 86)*. Turn left down the south-east ridge of Gillean and cross the lowest point at 2,408 feet after a quarter mile walk. Continue more interestingly along the top of a crescent-shaped cliff at the head of which stands the summit. Just before this hands will be employed over the topmost rocks.

90. SGÙRR BEAG
FROM BEALACH A' GHLAS-CHOIRE 2W

Sligachan 5¼ miles   2,550ft of ascent

From the Bealach at 2,099 feet turn right (north) if using An Glas-choire approach and follow the crest of a broad easy ridge until in 300 yards one is faced with a rockier ridge running across one's path. Scramble up easy rock and go right (east) and the summit sill soon be reached.

SGÙRR NA H-UAMHA 2,416ft

This spectacular gabbro peak forms the true and worthy termination of the Cuillin Main Ridge. From the south, as far away as Elgol it peeps over the Druim nan Ramh revealing a fantastic rock pinnacle. Rearing from the floor of Harta Corrie and Glen Sligachan in one classic unbroken sweeping line, its slabs of rough gabbro challenge assaults on the west, south and east faces. Here the brave may enjoy 1,000 feet rock climbs graded 'Difficult' to 'Severe'. Of the whereabouts of the 'cave' which gives the peak its name I'm uncertain. The first ascent was made by Charles Pilkington's party in 1887 after MacKenzie had made an attempt over the North Ridge.

Perhaps their route through a 'break in the rocks on the Glen Sligachan side' is easier than the North Ridge, but the latter is the usual way and a competent party with a rope will find it a safe but exciting climb.

The summit is disappointingly spacious. A minor scree-field continues south for a hundred yards towards the precipice overlooking Harta Corrie and Sligachan Glen. The views are gratifying however. The unbroken walls of An Caisteal across Lota Corrie are impressive whilst the Blaven Group show to advantage above Sràth na Crèitheach to the south-east.

Descent of course is a matter of Hobson's Choice on the peak itself but beyond the Bealach one can choose between a traverse of Sgùrr Beag (see *Routes 89 and 90*) then the descent of the 'Tourist Route' (*Route 86*) and a straight descent of An Glas-choire (*Route 16*).

91. SGÙRR NA H-UAMHA, NORTH RIDGE RII
Sligachan 5¼ miles 2,450ft of ascent

From Bealach a' Glas-choire (*Route 16*) turn south (left) if approaching from Glen Sligachan along the north ridge. Almost immediately the rock climbing begins and difficulties are best tackled directly. Climbing lands one on a minor peak beyond the gap. The second 'crux' or step is more easily taken on the right or west flank. Then nothing intervenes before the broad summit.

92. NEAD NA'H-IOLAIRE 760ft 2W
Sligachan 2¼ miles 800ft of ascent

This lowly height is paid scant interest these days. Once it was a venue for climbers on 'off-days' who assailed the gullies. Its heathery gabbro can be reached by a tedious diversion of a mile from the Tourist Path.

The boggy Glen Sligachan backed by Marsco is the chief interest in the view.

BLAVEN AND CLACH GLAS

BELIG   2,310ft.

Route 93 North Ridge	Loch Ainort	2W
Route 94 South-west Ridge	Ainort, Slapin	2W
Route 95 South-east Ridge	Slapin	2W

GARBH-BHEINN   2,644ft.

Route 96 Druim Eadar Dà Choire	Ainort	3S
Route 97 North-east Ridge	Ainort, Slapin	2W/3S
Route 98 South-east Ridge	Slapin, Crèitheach	2W/3S

SGÙRR NAN EACH   2,350ft.

Route 99 East Ridge	Slapin	2W
Route 100 West Ridge	Slapin, Crèitheach	2W

CLACH GLAS   2,582ft

Route 101 North Ridge	Slapin, Crèitheach	RII
Route 102 South Ridge	Slapin, Crèitheach	RII

BLAVEN   3,044ft

Route 103 Normal Route	Slapin	2W
Route 104 South Ridge/West Face	Camasunary, Crèitheach	2W
Route 105 North Face	Slapin, Crèitheach	RII

Our account of the Black Cuillin is completed with a final chapter devoted to one of Scotland's favourite Munros and its sporty little neighbour. This group forms the eastern sector of gabbro mountains encircling the Coruisk Basin. Happy and memorable days have been spent here by mountain folk of all abilities doing their special thing; walking, scrambling or climbing 'Extremely Severe' rocks. The northern outliers provide worthwhile 'off day' sport - or easy days from the roads around Lochs Ainort or Slapin in pathless secluded terrain.

Blaven from Am Bàsteir (Diagram p.132)

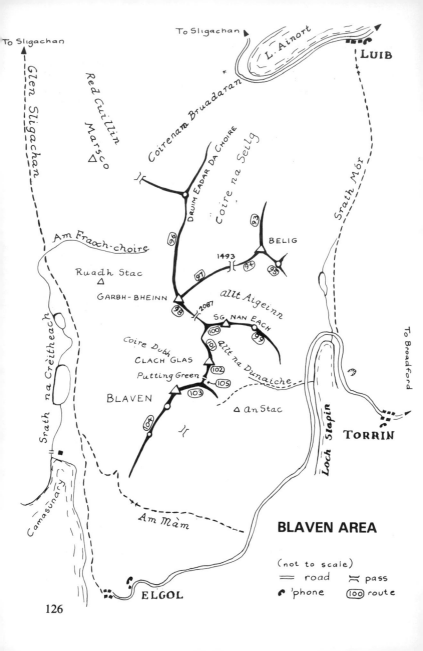

BLAVEN AREA

(not to scale)
= road   ⊐⊏ pass
☏ 'phone   ⑩ route

126

WESTERN APPROACHES 2W

There is easy access to the gaps between Garbh-bheinn/Sgùrr nan Each 2,087 feet, and Clach Glas/Blaven ('The Putting-Green' 2,280 feet) from the Sligachan-Camasunary path (*Route 3*). Head for Coire Dubh over moraines from Loch an Athain along the true right bank of the stream. The 2,087 col lies on the line of the stream and is reached up an easy head-wall of scree. The 'Putting Green' lies up a tributary branching right at 700 feet. Follow this below and between the rock faces of the two mountains. The final slopes are scree. 1½ miles from the path to Bealachs.

NORTHERN APPROACHES 1W

The verges of the A850 road that sweeps round the lonely head of Loch Ainort past the picturesque Eas a'Bhradain (Robbers' Fall), provide starting points for the valleys and ridges leading to Garbh-bheinn and Belig. The Bealach na Béiste 1,493ft, between, is gained by easy but soggy walking up Coire na Seilg up the east bank of Abhain Ceann Loch Ainort. A narrow and steeper branch valley enters from the left at some falls. Follow this past another wooded cataract - Eas a'Chait and the line of an old fence is crossed 100 feet below the pass, 1,493ft, 2 miles from the road. The other valley approach, Coire nam Bruadaran, above the Eas a'Bhradain leading to the north end of Garbh-bheinn is simple. A vague track along the south-east bank makes the driest start.

EASTERN APPROACHES 1-2W

Another A-class road - the A881 Broadford-Elgol road provides the most popular starting point for Blaven's Hills. This road does not slice across the landscape in the manner of the Broadford-Sligachan road but blends into a more picturesque landscape, partly inhabited and wooded at the head of a shaplier sea-loch Slapin. From the tarmac on the west shore two corries penetrate the range. The Allt Aigeinn gives simple steep walking to (a) Bealach na Béiste, 2 miles 1,493 feet between Garbh-bheinn and Belig. (b) Garbh-bheinn and Sgùrr nan Each col, 2½ miles 2,087feet. Easy scree runs give access to the ridge from the peaty hollow at 700 feet, drained by the Allt nan Dunaiche. A well worn path follows the north side of this stream. From the end of a disused fence a v-shaped valley - Choire a' Càise leads to a bowl of scree. The broad upper branch to the right leads to the western end of Sgùrr nan Each 100 feet above and south of the 2,087 feet easy col between Garbh-bheinn and Sgùrr nan Each. A narrow scree branch on the left leads to the lowest point between Sgùrr nan Each and Clach Glas 2,080 feet 2½ miles. N.B. This col is not a pass as the gully leading west down the other side is Arch Gully - a 'Moderate' rock climb! Between these screes lies Bealach Buttress giving climbing approaches to the right. At the head of the peaty hollow rears the East Face of Clach Glas. Stay immediately to the left on a westerly course below the turreted north face of Blaven and ascend scree to the 'Putting Green' the grassy col between Blaven and Clach Glas at 2,280 feet 2½ miles from the road.

BELIG 2,310ft.

This peak contains the northern limits of the Cuillin gabbro, which reaches half-way up the West Ridge. The rest of the hill is mostly basalt. No climbs have been reported on the crags of the north face. The view of Raasay (island) over Caol Mór is interesting. The simplest way down is the South-west Ridge.

93. BELIG - NORTH RIDGE 2W
Loch Ainort 2 miles   2,300ft. of ascent

The north gable end is reached over Coire Choinnich. The gabbro rocks may be avoided on the right (west) but regain the crest. Above 1,700 feet the basaltic ridge is well defined with crags to left and scree to right.

94. BELIG - SOUTH-WEST RIDGE 2W
Loch Ainort 2½ miles   2,300ft of ascent
Loch Slapin 2½ miles   2,300ft of ascent

From Bealach na Béiste a broad ridge is ascended over screes. Outcrops give no problem. The old march fence joins the ridge half-way and conducts you on this 800 feet climb over the top.

95. BELIG - SOUTH-EAST RIDGE 2W
Loch Slapin 2 miles   2,300ft of ascent

From the head of the loch take the west bank of the river draining Srath Mòr. The shingle of a tributary is crossed before heading left and up to the base of a steep ridge at 500ft with outcrops turned if needed to the left, avoiding the complex east face. 1,200 feet of unrelenting climbing fetches you to the 2,084 feet east end of the ¼ mile summit ridge overlooking the scree and rock north face. Cross a broad subsidiary top (2,113 feet) then ascend the last 200 feet of ridge where the old fence appears from the right off the top of a crag to conduct you to the summit.

GARBH-BHEINN 2,644ft.

This central peak is mainly gabbro. The northern end of Druim Eadar Dà Choire is granophyre. An extensive line of 500 feet high unexplored cliffs on the Coire na Seilg side runs below the North Ridge. Any one of the three ridges is a suitable way down. The south-west flank is simple but leads to the remote Srath na Crèitheach. The summit is the culmination of a good anti-clockwise walkers' horse-shoe incorporating Belig from Loch Ainort or another from Loch Slapin involving Belig and Sgùrr nan Each.

96. DRUIM EADAR DÀ CHOIRE 3S
Eas a' Bhradain 3¼ miles   2,800ft of ascent

The 1,605 feet summit of the Druim (2½ miles) can be reached along the broad then steep north end of the bealach at the head of Coire nam Bruadaran. The climb from this bealach is a broad 500 feet ridge accompanied by the old fence. 200 feet are lost on a similar descent south-east to the start of the North Ridge proper. This is a slightly rockier proposition and narrows when the fence ends 3-400 feet higher. The rocky summit ridge runs east-west. When it is engaged swing left to the top.

97. GARBH-BHEINN - NORTH-EAST RIDGE 3S
Lochs Ainort or Slapin 3 miles   2,700ft of ascent

Bealach na Bèiste lies at the foot of the ridge. The first 700 feet is broad and scree. The last 450 feet is interestingly narrow and rocky finishing abruptly at the summit.

98. GARBH-BHEINN - SOUTH-EAST RIDGE 3S
Loch Slapin 2½ miles 2,700ft of ascent

From the 2,087 feet bealach a simple 600 feet ⅓ mile ascent takes the well defined rocky ridge directly to the summit. The east (right) flank is steeper than the west.

SGÙRR NAN EACH 2,350ft.

Somewhat overshadowed this peak is often climbed as a pleasant

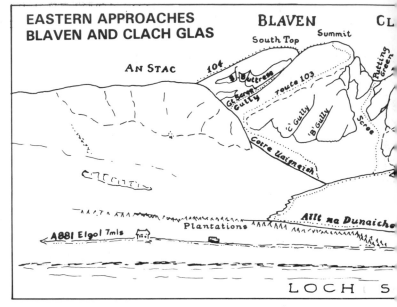

EASTERN APPROACHES
BLAVEN AND CLACH GLAS

BLAVEN   CL

South Top   Summit

An Stac   104   B Buttress
Gt Scree Gully   Toute 103
'C' Gully   'B' Gully   Scree
Putting Green

Coire Uaigneich

Allt na Dunaiche

Plantations

A881 Elgol 7mls

LOCH   S

approach to the classic Clach Glas-Blaven traverse. Easy practice in handling gabbro is afforded over the summit and west flank. Basalt appears on the east side except for the south-east ridge and east flank which is a complex of gritstones, granite, shale and more basalt. The 500 feet rock face on the north has a prominent ridge climbed by Harold Raeburn in 1898.

99. SGÙRR NAN EACH - EAST RIDGE 2W
Loch Slapin 2¼ miles 2,400ft of ascent

Follow the much used path along the north bank of the Allt na Dunaiche for a mile then head up and right up a vague ridge until at 1,100 feet the steeper, rockier rounded east end continues the ascent narrowing and circling left to avoid the head of a gully on the east face just below the East Top (2,035 feet 1¾ miles). The broad summit ridge dips 70 feet above a continuous broad scree-run cleaving the rocks of the north face. A gradual climb leads to the main top a quarter mile beyond the East Top.

130

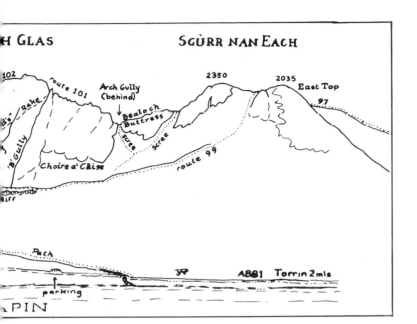

Labels in image: 102, route 101, Arch Gully (behind), Bealach Buttress, scree, scree, Choire a' Càise, route 99, 2350, 2035, East Top, 97, "'s" Rake, 'a' Gully, Cliff, Path, A881 Torrin 2 mls, parking, PIN

100. SGÙRR NAN EACH - WEST RIDGE 2W

Loch Slapin 2¾ miles 2,400 ft of ascent

The ½ mile of ridge between the Arch Gully dip to the summit running north-east then east is undulating, rocky but simple. Two bumps occur above Bealach Buttress. At the head of Choire a' Càise the connection with the 2,087 col runs north-north-west on a descending traverse of the slope. The ridge now rises more effectively to the West Top (2,323 feet) then a dip (2,150 feet) and a broad bump are closely succeeded by the summit.

CLACH GLAS 2,582ft.

One of the more shapely and entertaining mountains - Ashley Abraham entitled it 'the Matterhorn of Skye'. It is superior in one respect at least to its Alpine big brother - the rock is sound gabbro. The ridge is completely dissected by two dykes of dolerite or basalt running north-west - south-east and layered between dolerite

131

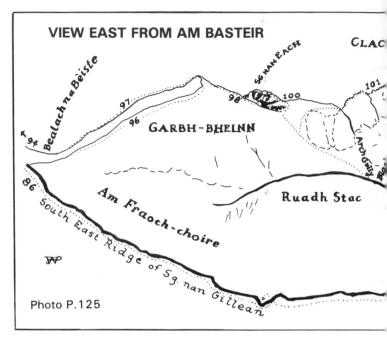

VIEW EAST FROM AM BASTEIR

Bealach na Bèiste

97

96

94

86

South East Ridge of Sg. nan Gillean

Am Fraoch-choire

GARBH-BHEINN

SG NAN EACH

98

100

CLAC

101

Arch Gully

Ruadh Stac

W

Photo P.125

sheets inclined Coruisk-wards creating ledges on the Slapin face. The slabs on the west face provide routes of 'Very Difficult'. The prominent Black Cleft Gully runs up to a tower north of the summit and is unclimbed. Another gully leading to the ridge on the south side of the peak was taken by Pilkington's party on the first ascent of the mountain and is graded 'Easy' by rock climbers. The east face's two dykes give gully climbs 'Very Difficult' (South) and 'Difficult'. A relative of Jack's Rake discovered by Sidney Williams gives the easiest route up this face beginning left of the south or 'A' gully which it crosses before attaining the ridge at the top of the north 'B' gully. The shortest, simplest descent takes the South Ridge to the 'Putting-Green', whence scree-runs lead to Sràth nan Créitheach or Loch Slapin. However, the continuation to Blaven is the standard finish to one of Scotland's top ten mountain days.

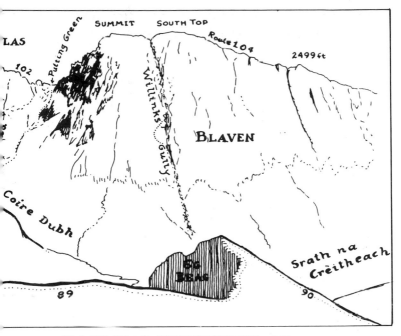

101. CLACH GLAS - NORTH RIDGE RII

Loch Slapin 2½ miles, Sligachan 7 miles
2,700ft of ascent

Beyond the col above Arch Gully and the narrow scree gully approach direct from Choire a' Caise: climb 150 feet to some pinnacles which are turned on the right (west). A wide stony gully is reached before the final peak. Across and below one's standpoint. a smaller gully in the opposite wall leads to steep broken rocks which provide a worthy climbing finish to the mossy summit rocks.

102. CLACH GLAS - SOUTH RIDGE and 'IMPOSTER' RII

Loch Slapin 2 miles, Sligachan 7 miles
2,600ft of ascent

The Blaven/Clach Glas bealach is known as the 'Putting Green',

2,280 feet. From this verdant hollow the climb begins its 300 yard 500 feet ascent bypassing some steps on the ridge including the Bealach Tower on the right. A larger vertical cliff is avoided by a traverse left to a steep gully with an awkward pitch. Beyond, the ridge levels until you are confronted by the Imposter - so called by the first climbers who smoked a pipe over this problem ahead. However, a short and steep but simple climb where the basalt creating the overhang cuts the skyline on the right establishes you on the sloping roof. The gradient of the rough slabs above the fraudulent rocks proves unexpectedly gentle on the short climb to the airy summit ridge a few strides south of the cairn.

BLÀ BHEINN, BLATH BHEINN, BLAVEN 3,044ft.

A mountain not to be missed by the fell walker. Its superlative situation and superb panorama are also the reward of the rock climber seeking the most difficult and spectacular routes in Scotland. A hill then for everyone with its high quality routes popular or remote!

Like Clach Glas, Blaven is chiefly gabbro sliced horizontally by sheets of dolerite but where the basalt dykes cross the broad northern end of the mountain, they complicate this high face where huge pinnacles have been weathered - the playground of the contemporary extreme climber. Coire Uaigneich has a granophyre base running between the basalt of the lower slopes of the east face and An Stac 1,729 feet.

The summit is distinguished from the South Top (3,032 feet 300 yards away towards Camasunary) by its triangulation pillar.

The simplest and shortest way to a road is the 'Normal' route from Loch Slapin. The scree gully dropping north-west to the Srath na Crèitheach can be used by parties making for Sligachan. This Long Gully (1,900 feet) was used by the Willink Brothers on their pioneering expedition. A steep pitch half way was avoided on the slabs to the left.

103. BLAVEN, THE NORMAL ROUTE 2W
Loch Slapin 2 miles 3 furlongs 3,100ft of ascent

Driving from Broadford past the turquoise - (deposits from Torrin marble quarry works creating this effect) - hued waters of Slapin steer around the head of the loch and park in the gravel pit over-

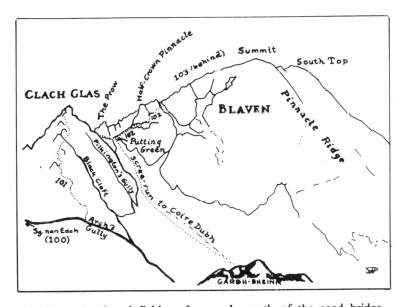

Map labels: CLACH GLAS, The Prow, Half-Crown Pinnacle, 103 (behind), Summit, South Top, 102, Pilkington's Gully, Putting Green, BLAVEN, Pinnacle Ridge, Black Cleft, Scree run to Coire Dubh, 101, Arch? Gully, Sg. nan Each (100), GARBH-BHEINN

looking abandoned fields a few yards south of the road bridge across Allt na Dunaiche and before a plantation. Re-cross the bridge and take the path on the true left bank of the river above its pleasant wooded waterfalls. After a mile of easy, sometimes boggy going, the path crosses the stream and an old fence. Continue over peat then heathery moraines to cross a tributary where it emerges between rocky walls. The path avoids these, climbing steeply up the right-hand grassy slopes of Coire Uaigneich and traversing beneath the crags of the east face. This climbing ground, explored in the early decades of this century, is cleft by C and D gullies between which runs a 'Difficult' buttress. Beyond here, double back out of a hollow and climb the ridge above. Promontories jut out over the rocky face on the right. At a dip at 2,600 feet the ridge steepens, narrows and adopts a leftward course for 300 feet before swinging right for the last easy broad 150ft climb to the Trig Pillar.

An alternative route used in 1873 on the Willink brothers ascent *from Broadford* is to continue into the upper reaches of Coire Uaigneich then climb the broad couloir of scree. (Great Gully) to the gap, 2,940 feet between the twin tops of the mountain. The left wall of this couloir is the South Buttress and boasts several 600 feet climbs at all standards. The smaller crags opposite are known as the South East Buttress with one 'Moderate' climb.

104. BLAVEN - THE SOUTH (CAMASUNARY) RIDGE
2W

Camasunary 2½ miles   3,200ft
Elgol 6 miles   3,500ft of ascent
Kirkibost 4 miles   3,600ft of ascent

This pleasant stroll was the means by which a poet - one Algernon Swinburne and Professor Nicol made the first visit to the summit.

200 yards east of Camasunary the Kirkibost/Elgol track bridges the Abhainn nan Leac. Follow its left (true right) bank for half a mile to a point where the Kikibost-Sligachan path by-passes Camasunary. Continue upstream beyond two waterfalls then head straight up the slope on the left to emerge on the rounded South Ridge at 1,200 feet. Minor bumps occur at 1,780 feet, 2,020 feet, 2,110 feet and 2,499 feet. Now and then a swing right avoids the heads of gullies slicing the north-east flanks. A less inspiring alternative is the continuation of Abhainn nan Leac to its source. Turn left up the south-east flank of the mountain avoiding the South Buttress over on the right (east). 100 yards beyond the South Top the ridge takes a 50 feet step (go left if necessary) to a col (2, 940 feet) and the final simple 180 yards to the Trig Pillar.

105. BLAVEN, NORTH FACE RII

Loch Slapin 2¼ miles   3,100ft of ascent
Sligachan 7½ miles   3,200ft of ascent

This route is the culmination of the classic traverse of Clach Glas (*Route 101 and Route 102*) and Blaven.

From the Putting Green 2,280 feet, easily but arduously gained from either Coire Dubh or Loch Slapin via scree shoots, you are confronted by 400 feet high rocks barring access to the ordinary route on the East Ridge. To the right a steep wall of 12-15 feet with big holds leads to a scree amphitheatre. The wall above is part of a large pinnacle. Go right along its base passing a steep chimney then turn sharp left up a scree-shoot to an enclosed platform west of the base of the Half Crown Pinnacle or the Horn. Climb a stone filled chimney straight ahead to the upper part of a scree gully leading to the east ridge at 2,600 feet. The rest of the way to one of the finest views imaginable is a pleasant walk.

136

APPENDIX I

GLOSSARY OF GAELIC AND NORDIC NAMES
With approximate pronunciation for Sassenachs

Abhainn Camas Fionnairigh (Avan Camasunary)   River Look-out Bay or Fair Sheiling.

Abhainn nan Leac (Lek)   River of Slabs.

a'Cioch (ah Hee-och)   The Breast.

Allt Aigeinn   Burn of the Abyss.

Allt a' Chaoich (Allt ah Kay oh ich)   Burn of the Foaming

Allt a' Ghlais-choire (Glais corrie)   Burn of the Grey Corrie.

Allt a' Mhaim (ah vyme)   Burn of the Hill, Moor.

Allt a' Mheadhoin (Veyatoin)   Central Burn.

Allt a' Mhuilinn (ah voolin)   Burn of the Mill.

Allt an Fhamhair (an averr)   Burn of the Giant

Allt an Uchd Buidhe (ucht boo-ee)   Burn of the Gold Breast

Allt Dearg Beag (jerrak-beg)   Small Red Burn

Allt Dearg Mòr (jerrak-more)   Big Red Burn

Allt Daraich (Daraich)   Timber Burn

Allt Fiaclan Dearg (Feeuchlan jerrak)   Red Teeth Burn

Allt na h-Airigh Leith (na-airy-lay-ee)   The Halfway Shelter Burn

Allt na Dunaiche   Burn of Misfortune

Allt na Meassaroch (mayassaroch)   Burn of Barreness

Allt nan Clachan Geala (gay-ahla)   Burn of the Bright Stones

Allt nan Fraoich-Choire   Heather Valley Burn

Allt Coire etc...   See under appropriate coire, corrie name

Am Bàsteir (am Barsiter)   The Executioner

Am Fraoch-choire (Frayoch-Horrie)   The heathery corrie

Am Màm (am m'am)   The Hill

An Caisteal (an caisteal)   The Castle

An Dorus (Un Dorrush)   The Door

An Garbh-choire (Un garrah-horry)   The Rough. Corrie

An Glas-choire   The Grey Corrie

An Sgùman (Un Skooman)   The Stack

An Stac   The Stack

Bealach a' Béiste (Bayeesta)   Pass of the Beasts

Bealach a' Bhàsteir (Bay-allach a Barsiter)   Pass of the Executioner

Bealach a' Garbh-choire (Bay-allach a garrah horry)   Pass of the Rough Corrie

Bealach a' Ghlas-choire (Bay-allach a glas-corrie)   Pass of the Grey Corrie

Bealach a' Mhaim (a vyme)   Pass over the moor

Bealach Coir' a' Ghrunnda (Corrie a' hroonda)   Pass of the Floor Corrie

Bealach Mhic Choinnich (Vick-ho-innich)   Mackenzie's Pass

Bealach na Glaic Moire (Gleyk More)   Pass of the Great Defile

Bealach nan Lice (Leeka)   Pass of the Flat Stones

Bealach Sgumain (Skoomain)   Pass of the Stack

Belig   Hill of the Birchbark

Bidein Druim nan Ramh (Bitjin Drim nan raav)   Sharp Peaks of the Ridge of Oars

Blà Bheinn (Blaven)   Blue Mountain

Bruach na Frithe (Brew-ach na free)   Brae of the Forest

Buaile Dhubh (Boo-ally doo)   Black Cattle Fold

Bualintur (Boo-allin-tur)   Tower Settlement

Caisteal a' Garbh-choire (garrah-horry)   Castle of the Rough Corrie

Camas Fhionnairigh (Camasunary)   Fair Shieling or Look-out Bay

Clach na Craoibhe Chaoruinn (Kray oh ee Kayorin)   Boulder of the enchanted tree (Rowan)

Clach Glas   Grey Rock

Cnoc Leathan (k-nock lay-un)   Broad Knoll

Coir' a' Chaoruinn (Kay or ruin)   Corrie of the rowan

Coir' a' Chruidh (croo-ee)   Corrie of the Cattle

Coir' a' Ghobhain (go-vain)   The Blacksmith's Corrie

Coir' a' Mhadaidh (vatee)   Fox's Corrie, coombe or cwm

Coir' an Eich (Un ey-ich   Horse Corrie

Coir' an Lochain   Corrie of the Loch

Coir' an Uaigneis (oo-arg nish)   Corrie of Solitude

Coir' - Uisg (Coruisk)   Cauldron of the Waters

Coire a' Bhàsteir (Barsitter)   Corrie of the Executioner

Coire a' Càise (Careesa)   Corrie of Rushing or Falling

Coire a'Ghredaidh (Cah-hreetah)   Corrie of the Storms

Coire a' Ghrunnda (a-hroonda)   The Bare or Floor Corrie

Coireachan Ruadha (corrie akkin roo-ah)   Ruddy Corries

Coire an t Seasaich (antee-a-sake)   Corrie of Barreness

Coire Beag (Beg)   Little Corrie

Coire Dubh (Doo)   Black Corrie

Coire Làgan (Lar-gan)   Corrie or Hollow Corrie

Coire na Circe (Keer-keh)   Corrie of the Hen

Coire na Creiche (hreesher)   Corrie of the Spoil or Booty
Coire nam Bruadaran   Corrie of Dreaming
Coire nan Allt Geala (gay-arler)   Corrie of the Sparkling Burn
Coire na Laogh (lay-oh)   Corrie of the Calf
Coire na Seilg   Corrie of the Hunted
Coire Riabach (reea-vuch)   Brindled Corrie
Coire Uaigneich   Hidden Corrie
Cuillin   The Coolin
    Cuchullin   Celtic - Irish - Gaelic God. Name popular in 19th
      Century
    A'Chuilionn. Gaelic   Holly
    Quillin   Alternative form of above
    Coolin. Old Welsh   Worthless
    Kjölen Norse Keel (of boat) or Mountain Ridge
    The anglicised plural form 'Cuillins' is erroneous!
Culnamean (cool nan may an)   end or Head of the Small Place

Druim Hain   Ridge of the Hinds
Druim nan Ramh (Raav)   Ridge of the Oars
Druim Eadar Da Choire (Ay a da-da horrie)   Ridge between
  two corries

Eag Dubh (Eck-doo)   Black Rift or Gash
Eas a'Bhradain (Vratain)   Fall of the Robbers
Eas a'Chait (Cat))   Cat
Eas Mór (Eyas more)   Great Cascade
Eileann Glas (Ellen glass)   Great Island
Eileann Reamhar (Rayavar)   Fat Island
Elgol (Norse)   Noble Dale

Fionn Choire   Fair Corrie

Garbh-bheinn (garaven)   Rough Mountain
Gars-bheinn (garsven) Echoing Hill
Glac Mhór (vore)   Great Hollow or Defile
Glen Brittle ?

Harta Corrie   Corrie of the Hart

Kyleakin   Haakon's Strait

Leachd Thuilm (lekt hoolim)   Slope, Hillside of Tulm
Loch Coruisk   Lake of the Corrie of Waters
Loch Dubh (Doo)   Dark Lake, Black Lake
Lochan Dubha (Doo-a)   Black Lakes
Loch an Fhir-bhaillaich (eer-va-ill-ach)   Lake of the Speckled
   Folk (trout)
Loch na Crèitheach (crayeeayach)   Lake of the Swamps
Loch na Cuilce (coo-ill-keh)   Lake of the Reeds
Loch na Leachd (lay-acht)   Lake of the Hillside
Loch Slapin   Muddy Loch
Lòn Bàn (lone barn)   White Marsh
Lota Corrie   Lofty Corrie

Meall a' Mhaim (may-all a vyme)   Hill of the Pass
Meallan Dearg (may-all an jerrak)   Red Hills
Meall Dearg (may-all jerrak)   Red Hill
Meall Odhar (oh-ah)   Dappled Hill
Meall nan Cuilce (koo-ill-keh)   Hill of the Reeds

Nead na'h-Iolaire (nay-add na yowlair)   The Eagle's nest

Portree   Kings' Harbour
Port Sgàile (Scar-eela)   Shadow Bay

Ruadh Stac (roo-ah stack)   Ruddy Stack
Rubh' a' Gheodha Buidhe (roova heeova vooy) Yellow Check
   Point
Rubha Bàn (roova Barn)   White Point
Rubha buidhe (booy)   Yellow Point
Rubha Port Sgaìle (sgar-illy)   Shadow Harbour Point

Scavaig (Norse) Gloomy Bay
Sgeir Dorcha (skerry-dorka)   Hidden Shoal
Sgùrr a' Bhasteir (Skoor-a-Basitter)   Peak of the Executioner
Sgùrr a'Choire Bhig (vick)   of the Little Corrie
Sgùrr a'Fionn Choire (fee-un)   of the Fair Corrie
Sgùrr a'Ghreadaidh (hreetay)   of the Storms or Clear Waters
Sgùrr a'Mhadaidh (vatee)   of the Fox
Sgùrr an Fheadain (aityan)   of the Waterpipe
Sgùrr Alasdair (allister)   Alexander's Peak
Sgùrr Beag (beg)   Small Peak

Sgùrr Coir'an Lochain   Peak of the Corrie Loch
Sgùrr Dearg (jerrak)   Red Peak
Sgùrr Dearg Beag (jerrak beg)   Little Red Peak
Sgùrr Dubh Beag (skoor doo beg)   Little Black Peak
Sgùrr Dubh Mòr (doo more)   Large Black Peak
Sgùrr Dubh na Da Bheinn (doo na da ven)   Black Peak of the
   Two Mountain(s) Ridges
Sgùrr Eadhar Da Choire   Peak between Two Corries
Sgùrr Hain   Peak of the Hinds
Sgùrr Mhic Choinnich (vick-hoe-innich)   Mackenzie's Peak
Sgùrr Sgumain (Skooman)   Stack Peak
Sgùrr Thearlaich (hearlake)   Charles' Peak. (C.E. Pilkington)
Sgùrr Thuilm (hoolim)   Tulm's Peak. (Gaelic Hero)
Sgùrr Thormaid (horrer-madge)   Norman's Peak.
                                           (Prof. N.J.Collie)
Sgùrr na Banachdich   Smallpox Peak
Sgùrr na Bannachaig   Milkmaid's Peak - Alternative of
   Banachdich
Sgùrr na Bhairnich (vairnich)   Limpet Peak
Sgùrr na Uamha (oo-ah va)   Peak of the Cave
Sgùrr na Stri   Peak of Strife (winds)
Sgùrr nan Each (Ay-ach)   Peak of the Horses
Sgùrr nan Eag (Eck)   Peak of the Chasm or Cleft
Sgùrr nan Gillean (hard 'g', emphasise 1st syllable)   Peak of young
   men, or Gills (N).
Sgùrr nan Gobhar (go-ar)   Peak of the Goat
Skye or Ant-Eilean Sgitheanach   The Island of the Sky
   Eilean-a-Cheo   Island of Mist
Sligachan   Place of Shells
Soay   Swine, Goat, Island
Sràth na Crèitheach (shrah na cray ee ach)   Valley of the Bogs
Srath Mór   Great Valley
Sròn na Ciche (shrone na kee sher)   Shoulder or Hump of the
   Breast.
Sròn Dearg (shrone jerrak)   Red Shoulder

Tobar na Uaislean (oo·ais·lay·an)   Well of the Gentrymen

A LIST OF 67 TOPS ON, OR ADJOINING THE CUILLIN MAIN RIDGE.

MUNRO SUMMITS 11
Munro Tops 9
Other 3,000ft peaks 3
2,000-3,000ft peaks & tops 32
Under 2,000 12

	EASIEST ROUTE	FEET	METRES	ROUTES
Sg. ALASDAIR	4S	3257	993	(37-38)
INACCESSIBLE PINNACLE	RII	3234	986	(50-51)
Sg. Dearg	3S	3209	978	(47-49)
Sg. Thearlaich	RI	3208	978	(32-35)
SG. A'GHREADAIDH	4S	3192	973	(58-60)
South Top, Sg. a'Ghreadaidh	4S	3181	969	(59)
SG. NAN GILLEAN	4S	3167	965	(86-88)
SG. NA BANACHDICH	2W	3166	965	(52-55)
BRAUCH NA FRITHE	2W	3143	958	(75-77)
An Stac	4S	3130	954	(49)
SG. MHIC COINNICH	4S	3111	948	(45-46)
Sg. Sgumain	2W	3108	947	(39-40)
SG. DUBH MÒR	4S	3096	944	(29-30)
South Peak, Sg. na Banachdich	4S	3089	942	(54)
Sg. Dubh na Da Bheinn	3S	3078	938	(26-28)
AM BÀSTEIR	RI	3069	935	(84-85)
Sg. a'Fionn Choire	3S	3068	935	(78)
Sg. Thormaid	3S	3040	927	(56-57)
Sg. Dearg Beag	2W	3040	927	(47)
SG. NAN EAG	2W	3031	924	(22-24)
Top Midget Ridge	3S	3023	921	(54)
SG. A'MHADAIDH	4S	3012	918	(61-63)
Basteir Tooth	RIII	3005	916	(82-83)
Knight's Peak	RIII	2994	912	(88)
Sg. a'Bhasteir	2W	2951	899	(79-81)
1st Peak, Sg. a'Mhadaidh	4S	2939	896	(63)
Gars-bheinn	1W	2935	895	(17-21)
3rd Peak, Sg. a'Mhadaidh	RII	2934	894	(63)
2nd Peak, Sg. a'Mhadaidh	RII	2910	887	(63)
3rd Pinnacle, Gillean	4S	2892	881	(88)
Sròn Bhuidh	2W	2887	880	(54)

	EASIEST ROUTE	FEET	METRES	ROUTES
Sg. Thuilm	2W	2885	879	(61)
Sg. a'Choire Bhig	2W	2872	875	(21-22)
Central Peak, Bidein Druim nan Ramh	RII	2850	869	(66-68)
Sg. na Bhairnich	4S	2826	861	(75)
Sròn na Ciche	2W	2817	859	(41-43)
North Top, Bidein	RII	2794	852	(67)
S-W Top Bidein	RII	2779	847	(67)
An Caisteal	4S	2724	830	(73-74)
Caisteal a' Garbh-choire	RII	2719	850	(25)
2nd Pinnacle, Gillean	3S	2655	809	(88)
Sg. Eadar da Choire	2W	2650	808	(60)
Sg. Beag	2W	2511	765	(89-90)
1st Pinnacle, Gillean	3S	2510	765	(88)
South Top, Sg. Coir' an Lochain	2W	2491	759	(36)
Druim Pinnacle	RII	2467	752	(68)
Sg. nah-Uamha	RII	2416	736	(91)
Sg. Dubh Beag	RII	2403	732	(30)
North Top, Sg. Coir' an Lochain	RII	2390	728	(36)
An Diallaid	2W	2340	713	(52)
A' Cioch	RII	2336	712	(43)
Sg. an Fheadain	2W	2253	687	(64-65)
Sròn Dearg	2W	2090	637	(47)
Meall Odhar	2W	2085	636	(81)
Sg. nan Gobhar	2W, 3S	2069	631	(53)
Sròn Tobar nan Uaislean	1W	1682	513	(77)
Druim nan Ramh	2W	1636	499	(68)
Sgùrr na Stri	2W	1631	497	(72)
Sgùrr Hain	1W	1386	422	(71)
Meall Dearg	1W	1196	365	(70)
Druim Hain	1W	1141	348	(70)
Meallan Dearg	1W	1060	323	(69)
An Sgùman	1W	806	246	(44)
Nead na' h-Iolaire	2W	760	232	(92)
Ceann na Beinne	2W	737	225	(44)
Meall na Cuilce	1W	590	180	(31)
Cnoc Leathan	1W	560	171	(43)

THE BLAVEN GROUP
Comprising 1 Munro Summit, 1 Munro Top

BLAVEN	2W	3044	928	(103-5)
S Top	2W	3032	924	(104)
Garbh-Bheinn	2W	2644	806	(96-8)
Clach Glas	RII	2582	787	(101-2)
Sgùrr nan Each	1W	2350	716	(99-100)
Belig	2W	2310	704	(93-5)
Druim Eadar Dà Choire	1W	1605	489	(96)

Printed by CARNMOR PRINT & DESIGN
95-97 LONDON ROAD, PRESTON, LANCASHIRE, UK.

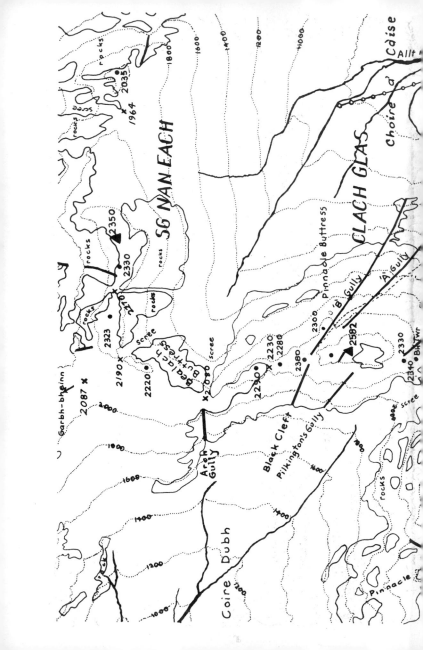